# THE WRITINGS OF
# ST FRANCIS OF ASSISI

# THE WRITINGS OF
# ST FRANCIS OF ASSISI

*Edited by*
**Halcyon Backhouse**

**HODDER AND STOUGHTON**
LONDON  SYDNEY  AUCKLAND

**DEDICATION**

For my sister
Cleoné Ninnette De L'ange Prins

Copyright © 1994 Halcyon Backhouse

The right of Halcyon Backhouse to be identified as the Editor of
the Work has been asserted by her in accordance with the
Copyright, Designs and Patents Act 1988.

First published in Great Britain 1994
by Hodder and Stoughton

10 9 8 7 6 5 4 3 2

British Library Cataloguing in Publication Data

A catalogue record for this title is available
from the British Library

ISBN 0 340 60594 4

Typeset by
Watermark, Cromer, Norfolk NR27 9HL

Printed and bound in Great Britain by
Cox & Wyman Ltd, Reading, Berkshire

Hodder and Stoughton
A Division of Hodder Headline PLC
338 Euston Road
London NW1 3BH

# CONTENTS

**Part III** *The Office of the Lord's Passion*

**Part IV** *Prayers and Canticles*
**Prayers**

**Canticles**

# FOREWORD TO THE 1994 EDITION

Francis of Assisi, 1181/2–1226, is remembered for being the founder of the Franciscans. His father, Pietro Bernardone, was a wealthy cloth merchant in Assisi. As a result of a severe illness and because he became increasingly dissatisfied with his worldly life, Francis decided that he would give his life to caring for the poor and to prayer. During a pilgrimage to Rome, Francis was moved to the depths of his being by the sight of all the beggars outside St Peter's. For one day he exchanged his own clothes for those of one of the beggars and spent the day begging. Coming from such a well-off family, Francis was deeply affected by this experience of being penniless. When he returned home, his father would have nothing more to do with him and Francis spent his days in repairing the ruined church of St Damiano and in looking after lepers.

One day, while Francis was worshipping God in St Damiano church, he listened intently as the words of Jesus Christ from Matthew chapter 10 verses 7–19 were read:

*And as ye go, preach, saying, The kingdom of heaven is at hand. Heal the sick, cleanse the lepers, raise the dead, cast out devils: freely ye have received, freely give. Provide neither gold, nor silver, nor brass in your purses; Nor scrip for your journey, neither two coats, neither shoes, nor yet staves: for the workman is worthy of his meat. And into whatsoever city or town ye shall enter, inquire who in it is worthy; and there abide till ye go thence. And when ye come into a house, salute it. And if the house be worthy, let your peace come upon it: but if it be not worthy, let your peace return to you. And whosoever shall not receive you, nor hear your words, when ye depart out of that house or city, shake off the dust of your feet. Verily I say unto you, It shall be more tolerable for the land of Sodom and Gomorrah in the day of judgement, than for that city.*

*Behold, I send you forth as sheep in the midst of wolves: be ye therefore wise as serpents, and harmless as doves. But beware of men: for they will deliver you up to the councils, and they will scourge you in their synagogues; And ye shall be brought before governors and kings for my sake, for a testimony against them and the Gentiles. But when they deliver you up, take no thought how or what ye shall speak: for it shall be given you in that same hour what ye shall speak.*

Francis took these words of his Lord to heart and he knew that they were a personal call to him. He took them literally. He threw away his staff and removed his shoes and went about barefoot. He put on a long, black, hooded cloak which had just a simple cord for a belt. Then Francis set out to preach the gospel of our Lord Jesus Christ in his quest to save souls.

Before long, a group of like-minded people joined Francis who wrote a simple rule for life (*Regula Primitiva*), based on Jesus' sayings in the Gospels. The movement mushroomed and at the Chapter in Assisi on Pentecost day in 1217 the Order was organised into provinces with a supervising minister in charge of each province. Francis knew that his gift was not administration and organisation and he willingly relinquished the leadership of the movement as it grew.

Francis did not write a great deal. All his writings were

quite short in length. This edition of his collected works is based on Lady de la Warr's translation of 1907, which in turn was based on d'Alençon's French edition. Part of d'Alençon's introduction has been retained as it explains interesting background information about some of the individual items of Francis' writings. All the material enclosed in square brackets [ ] comes from Lady de la Warr's footnotes and these have been included whenever they throw light on Francis' writings or life. Lady de la Warr's use of the Douai translation of Bible quotations has been retained, but references have been altered where necessary to conform to the usage of modern English versions.

Today, Francis is thought of as 'the most lovable of all the saints'. As G.K. Chesterton put it, 'St Francis was a poet whose whole life was a poem.' He is remembered for his deep humility, his love of nature, his wholehearted devotion to God and man, his spirit of generosity, and perhaps most of all, for his quiet, simple trust in his Lord and Saviour.

*Halcyon Backhouse*
*Crostwight, 1993*

# FOREWORD TO THE 1907 EDITION

The minor works of St Francis of Assisi were translated into English for the first time, I think, in 1890, in London, by the Franciscans. This translation was from Wadding's celebrated text, whose Latin edition was published in Antwerp in 1623.

Since then two very important books have been published. They are *Opuscula sancti Patris Francisci Assisiensis sec. codices MSS. emendata et denuo edita a PP. Collegii S. Bonaventurae*, edited by L. Lemmens (Quaracchi, 1904); and, *Analekten zur Geschichte des Franciscus von Assisi: S. Francisci Opuscula,* edited by Dr H. Boehmer (Tübingen and Leipzig, 1904). Pascal Robinson was particularly indebted to Lemmens' work in the preparation of the very fine translation published in the United States of America (*The Writings of St Francis of Assisi* (Philadelphia, 1906)). It is fitting that England should possess a version of its own; and this is furnished in the present work, as the basis of which Lady de la Warr has done me the honour to use my critical French edition (Paris: Poussielgue, 1905).

E. d'Alençon, 1907

# D'ALENÇON'S INTRODUCTION
# TO THE 1907 EDITION

It is necessary to give some information about the documents which comprise the minor works of St Francis of Assisi.

## The Wadding edition

This celebrated edition contains the complete revelation of the mind of St Francis. Along with the authentic writings of St Francis Wadding inserted other people's writings. I have avoided inserting anything which does not faithfully represent the meaning of St Francis' writings.

## Rules

### Rules of the Friars Minor
The Rules of the Friars Minor was written three times: in 1209, in 1210–1221 and in 1223. The text of the first Rule we have dates from between 1210 and 1221.

After his conversion St Francis renounced his paternal inheritance. Followers grouped themselves around him and he found it necessary to give them a Rule or form of life. The holy gospel gave them daily spiritual nourishment. From it St Francis drew the substance to form his

Rule. 'My brothers,' he said to his companions, 'I see that God has been pleased to increase our numbers. Let us go to our Holy Roman Church and report what God has already wrought by our means, in order that we may continue, according to its will and under its orders, the work we have begun.' With this in mind, Francis visited Pope Innocent III who was full of good will towards the friars but declined to give his sanction to their manner of life. However, Cardinal John of St Paul persuaded him to change his mind. 'If we refuse', the cardinal said, 'the request of this poor man who asks permission to live according to the gospel, let us beware lest we set ourselves against the gospel itself; to hold that the complete observance of the gospel contains anything novel, unreasonable or impracticable is to blaspheme Jesus Christ, the Author of the gospel.'

Pope Innocent III hastened to grant the favour implored, blessed the brothers, openly approved their Rule of life and permitted them everywhere to preach repentance.

The text of the 1209 version of the Rule is lost. However Boehmer has tried to restore some of its lines as follows: 'I beg all of my brothers never in sickness to murmur nor to rebel against God or the other brothers; let them not be too anxious to find remedies, let them not seek with too great eagerness to relieve this flesh, which is the enemy of the soul and must soon die; but let them in everything give thanks and desire to live as God wills. Those indeed whom God predestines for eternal life he instructs and spurs on through tribulation and trial, according to his word, "Such as I love, I rebuke and chastise."' The text of the Rule written, modified and enlarged between 1210 and 1221 forms the first in this book.

Later, on November 29, 1223, a third Rule was drawn up for the written approbation of the Court of Rome. Today Franciscans of the first Order, Conventuals, Monks, Minors or Capuchins, observe this last Rule. For the two translations I have entirely followed Quaracchi. This edition gives the text of our second Rule according to the original papal Bull.

### Fragments addressed to St Clare

'When the most high celestial Father graciously deigned to illuminate my heart,' St Clare tells us in chapter four of her Rule, 'and caused me to repent on the advice and after the example of our blessed father, St Francis, a short time after his conversion, I and my sisters willingly promised him obedience. And seeing that we did not in the least fear poverty, labour, persecution, humility or the scorn of the age, but rather looked upon them with delight, the most blessed father, full of compassion, wrote for us a little rule of life.'

### Concerning the Religious Living in Hermitages

This fragment is useful for the insight it gives into the origin of the Franciscan movement. In the beginning, the brothers, few in number, had no permanent domicile; they dwelt either in leper-houses or in little temporary dwellings on the outskirts of the towns. The need for a place in which they could more freely give themselves up to a regular contemplative life, by degrees gave rise to the hermitage. It was for these houses, these *loci*, that St Francis made this little Rule. The increase in the number of the brothers, the desire to have a chapel of their own, the example given by the basilica of Assisi, developed this movement, and they soon had proper convents. It must be observed that St Francis never used the word *conventus*, but the word *locus*, to designate the abode of the brothers.

### The Testament

I do not think any other writing so truly reveals the mind of St Francis. In this last testament the saint lays bare his heart, his whole soul, his innermost being. He who had received the holy stigmata at Alvernia wrote it at the end of his life, and it was witnessed by Celano, his friend Ugolino and St Bonaventura.

## The Admonitions
It is not known when they were composed; but they are surely by St Francis. From the 13th century they are given as such in the MS in the Laurentian Library, at Florence. I revised my translation from a MS of the 15th century in the National Library of Paris.

## Letter to all Christians
The Latin text, translated here from the Quaracchi edition, was revised from the MSS in the Mazarin Library. It is sometimes given under the form of a letter, sometimes as an 'opusculum' or little treatise.

## Letter to the General Chapter
This letter brings us to the end of the life of St Francis and reveals his humility to the Church of Rome.

## Letter to a Minister
If one can trust the Italian versions of this letter, it is addressed to Brother Elias. Wadding thinks that the letter was addressed to Peter of Catana.

## Letter to Priests on the Holy Sacrament
Wadding heads this letter with the following words: 'To my spiritual lords in Christ, to all priests in the world who live according to the rules of the Catholic faith, Brother Francis, their lowest and most humble servant, sends greeting with the greatest respect and reverence. As I am every one's debtor and cannot, because of my infirmities, personally give you satisfaction, receive with all my love and charity this remembrance of me and this briefly written exhortation.' Wadding adds at the end, 'May our Lord Jesus Christ comfort all my masters and fill them with his holy grace.'

*Letter to the Guardians (1)*
The word 'custos' must here, as elsewhere, we think, be translated as 'guardian'.

*Letter to the Guardians (2)*
We have this letter on Wadding's authority alone, from a Spanish version, but as it agrees wonderfully with the other letters and as it is indisputably full of the spirit of St Francis, there is no reason to suspect the credulity of the old annalist.

*Letter to Brother Leo*
It is quite clear that, according to custom, greeting is sent from the writer to the person addressed. But in this instance (*F. Leo, F. Francisco tuo salutem et pacem*) the humility of St Francis makes him reverse this order, and beg of his dear and well-loved little sheep of the good God those blessings of which he feels in need.

*Little Letter to Brother Leo; or, Praises to God*
In this we have the precious possession of a holograph of St Francis.

*The Letter to Dame Jacqueline*
Edouard d'Alençon was the first to introduce us to this friend of St Francis. This is what Celano says about the fortunate receiver of this letter: 'Jacqueline of Settesoli, one of the principal ladies of the town of Rome, had, through her saintliness and nobility, gained the favour of a special friendship with the saint.' And continuing, the historian mentions the greatness of her house, the rank of her family, her great riches, and in a word the admirable perfection of her virtues through a long and austere widowhood.

*The Prayer for Poverty*
This prayer, which every devout novice of the Order

recites and which everyone knows, is not by St Francis. Its author is not known, but might nevertheless be John Parent or St Antony of Padua. In any case it is a masterpiece and a gem of Franciscan literature.

## The Office of the Passion

Through Celano we learn that St Francis composed an Office of the Passion, *Officium Crucis*. It divided into five parts:

1. For the three last days of Holy Week and the vigils during the year.
2. For the Paschal season.
3. For Sundays and festivals throughout the year.
4. For Advent.
5. For the feast of Christmas and the days following until the end of the octave of the Epiphany.

We translate it from the triple Latin editions of Wadding, Quaracchi and Boehmer.

# Part I

# RULES, TESTAMENTS AND ADMONITIONS

# RULES

## The Rule of the Friars Minor, 1210–1221

In the name of the Father, and of the Son, and of the Holy Spirit. Amen.

This is the rule of life which Brother Francis begged the Holy Father Innocent to grant and sanction. And the Pope blessed and confirmed it to him and his friars for ever.

That Brother Francis and all who shall be at the head of this Order promise reverence and obedience to the Holy Pope Innocent and his successors. And that the other brothers shall be bound to obey Brother Francis and his successors.

### 1 The friars shall live in obedience and chastity and without earthly goods

The rule and life of these friars is the following: to live in obedience and chastity and without property, and to follow the example and teaching of our Lord Jesus Christ, who says, 'If thou wilt be perfect, go, sell what thou hast and give to the poor, and thou shalt have treasure in heaven; and come, follow me' (Matt. 19:21). And again, 'If any man will come after me, let him deny himself, and take up his cross and follow me' (Matt. 16:24). And, 'If any man come to me and hate not his father and mother and wife and children and brethren and sisters, yea, and his own life also, he cannot be my disciple' (Luke 14:26).

'And every one that hath left father or mother, brothers or sisters, or wife, or children or lands, for my sake, shall receive an hundredfold and shall possess life everlasting' (Matt. 19:29).

## 2 Concerning the reception and the habit of friars

If anyone through divine inspiration desires to lead this life and comes to our friars, let him be received by them with kindness. If he persists in wishing to take up our life, let the friars be very careful not to meddle with his temporal affairs, and let them present him to their minister as soon as possible. And let the minister receive him with charity, and encourage him and explain to him with great care the manner of our life. That being done, the postulant, if he is willing and can do so honourably and without difficulty, must sell all his goods and distribute them among the poor. But the friars and the ministers of the friars must ever be on their guard against meddling in any way with these affairs; they must never receive any money either for themselves or for any intermediate person. If, however, they are in need, the friars may assuredly, like other poor people, receive things necessary for the body, but no money.

When the postulant has returned, let the minister give him the habit of probation for one year, that is to say, two tunics without hood, girdle, breeches and cape reaching to the girdle. The year of probation having elapsed, he may be received into obedience. After this he cannot change into another Order nor exempt himself from obedience according to the command of the Holy Father. For according to the Gospel, 'No man putting his hand to the plough, and looking back, is fit for the kingdom of God' (Luke 9:62). But if someone comes who cannot give away his goods without difficulty, but has the spiritual will to relinquish them, it shall suffice. That no man shall be received contrary to the form prescribed by Holy Church.

The other friars who have promised obedience shall

have a tunic with a hood and another without, if necessary, and the girdle and breeches. And all the brothers must be dressed in poor clothes which they can patch with bits of the same or other pieces, with the blessing of God, for the Lord says in the Gospel, 'They that are in costly apparel and live delicately and are clothed in soft garments are in the houses of kings' (cf. Luke 7:25).

And even if they should be called hypocrites, let them not cease therefore to be doing good; let them not seek rich garments in this world, in order that they may be clothed with glory in the kingdom of heaven.

### 3 Concerning the divine office and fasting

The Lord says: This kind of demons 'can go out by nothing, but by prayer and fasting' (Mark 9:28). And again, 'When you fast, be not as the hypocrites, sad' (Matt. 6:16). Therefore, let all the friars, clerks or lay brothers recite the divine office, lauds and prayers according to the prescribed form. [The services of each day began with Matins, immediately followed by Lauds; the other services were Prime, Terce, Sext, None, Vespers and Compline. – *1994 Editor's note*.] Let the clerks say the office for the living and for the dead, as other clerks do. Every day let them say the *Miserere mei, Deus* ('Lord, have mercy on me') and the *Pater noster* ('Our Father') for the failings and negligences of the friars; for deceased friars let them say the *De profundis* ('Out of the depths') and the *Pater noster*. And they may only possess the books necessary to perform their office. Lay brothers who know how to read may have a Psalter, the others who do not know how to read are to have no books. The lay brothers shall say the *Credo in Deum* ('I believe in God') and twenty-four Our Fathers and *Gloria Patris* ('Glory to the Father') for Matins; five for Lauds, the *Credo in Deum* and seven Our Fathers and Glorias for Prime; for Terce, Sext and None, seven for each and twelve for Vespers; the *Credo in Deum* and seven Our Fathers and glorias for Compline; seven

Our Fathers with the *Requiem aeternam* ('Rest eternal') for the dead; and three Our Fathers every day for the faults and negligences of the friars.

Likewise all the friars shall fast from the feast of All Saints until the Nativity of the Lord, and from the Epiphany, the period at which the fasting of our Lord Jesus Christ began, until Easter. At other times they shall not be obliged to fast except on Fridays, according to the Rule. And they may be allowed to eat of any food set before them, as is taught in the Gospel, 'When ye enter a town and are welcomed, eat what is set before you' (Luke 10:8).

### 4 Concerning the subjection of ministers and other friars

In the name of the Lord, let all the friars who are ministers and servants of the others establish their friars in their own provinces and places and let them visit them frequently to encourage and give them spiritual advice. And let all my other blessed friars obey them diligently in all that concerns the eternal salvation of the soul, and is not contrary to our Rule. And let them mutually observe the Saviour's words, 'All things therefore whatsoever you would that men should do to you, do you also to them' (Matt. 7:12), and, 'See thou never do to another what thou wouldst hate to have done to thee by another' (Tobit 4:16). And let the ministers who are servants remember these words of the Saviour, '[I am] not come to be ministered unto, but to minister' (Matt. 20:28). The souls of their friars have been entrusted to them, and if one of them through their fault or bad example is lost, they will have to give account before the Lord Jesus Christ at the day of judgement.

### 5 Correcting friars' faults

Watch diligently over your own souls and the souls of your friars, for it is fearful to fall into the hands of the living God (see Heb. 10:31). If one of the ministers should give a friar an order contrary to our Rule or to conscience, the friar is not bound to obey him, for there can be no question of obedience where there is fault or sin. Therefore, all the friars who are in subjection to the ministers or servants shall be on the watch to examine reasonably and diligently the conduct of the ministers and servants. And if they see one of them walking according to the world and not spiritually according to the perfection of our life, and if he does not amend after three admonitions, he must be deposed from his office of minister and servant of the whole fraternity, without exception, at the Chapter meeting at Pentecost, in spite of any obstacle that may be in the way. If among the friars, wherever they may be, there is one who wills to walk not according to the spirit but according to the flesh, let his companions, the other friars, warn him, reprove and reform him with care and humility. If he refuses to amend after the third admonition, the friars must report him to his minister or send him to him as soon as possible.

The minister and servant shall do with him what he judges most fit in the sight of God. And let all the friars, ministers and servants and others take great care not to worry themselves, nor to grow angry because of the sin or bad example of another, because the devil through the sin of one tries to corrupt many others. But let them come spiritually to the aid of the guilty one, as well as they can, for 'they that are in health need not a physician, but they that are ill' (Matt. 9:12).

Also the friars must not behave in an arrogant and domineering way, especially among themselves, for the Lord says in the Gospel, 'You know that the princes of the Gentiles lord it over them: and they that are the greater, exercise power upon them' (Matt. 20:25). It must not be so among friars, and 'he that is greatest among you, shall be your servant' (Matt. 23:11), and minister, and 'he that is the greater among you, let him become as the younger' (Luke 22:26).

No friar shall speak ill of or do harm to another; rather,

in holy charity let them willingly serve and obey one
another. This is the true and holy obedience of our Lord
Jesus Christ. And let the friars who have erred from the
ways of the Lord and rebelled against obedience know
that, as the Psalmist says, 'they are cursed who decline
from thy commandments' (Ps. 119:21), so long as they
deliberately remain in sin. But so long as they persevere in
the law of the Lord, which they have promised to do by
the holy gospel and their Rule, let them know that they
are keeping in true obedience and have the blessing of the
Lord.

## 6 The appeal of the friars to their ministers: no brother may be called prior

If the friars, in whatever place they are, cannot observe
our life, let them go as soon as possible to their minister
and lay their difficulties before him. Let the minister try to
help him as he himself would wish if he were in a similar
situation.

Let no one be called prior, but let everyone take the
name of friars minor. Let them wash one another's feet.

## 7 Serving and working

No friar, wherever he serves or works, shall ever be cham-
berlain, cellarer or steward. He shall not undertake any
work which is likely to bring harm to his soul. Let him be
subject to all who are in the same house.

Let the brothers who know how to work practise their
former trade if it is not harmful to their soul's salvation
and if it is convenient to do so. For the Psalmist says,
'Thou shalt eat the labours of thy hands: blessed art thou,
and it shall be well with thee' (Ps. 128:2). And the apostle
Paul writes, 'If any man will not work, neither let him eat'
(2 Thess. 3:10). And let each keep to the employment or
trade to which he was called (see 1 Cor. 7:24). In return
for work the brothers may receive the necessities of life,
but no money. If it is necessary, let them go and beg alms

like others. They are allowed to have the tools they need for their work.

Let all the friars endeavour to labour at an occupation which is good for the soul. For St Jerome has written, 'Be always doing some good work that the devil may not find thee idle.' And Anselm wrote, 'Idleness is the enemy of the soul.' Therefore the servants of God must always be at prayer or employed in doing some good work.

The friars must be on their guard, wherever they may be, in hermitages or other places, against appropriating any dwelling or driving another out. Whoever visits them, be he a friend or an enemy, a thief or a robber, must be welcomed with kindness. Wherever friars may be let them be diligent to respect and honour one another devoutly and without murmuring. Friars must take care not to be sad and dull like hypocrites. Rather they must be seen to be joyful in the Lord, having a cheerful face and filled with engaging amiability.

*8 The friars may never receive money*
The Saviour gives this precept in the gospel, 'Take heed, and beware of all malice and avarice, and guard yourselves from the solicitudes of this world and cares of this life' (see Luke 12:15 and 21:34). No friar shall, in any place where he is staying or passing through, take, receive or even cause to be received coins or money of any kind. A friar is not allowed to buy clothes or books or to receive them in payment for work. Only in cases of absolute necessity for sick brothers can an exception be made to this.

We must not value or esteem money or coins more than stones. The devil will blind the eyes of those who desire and appreciate money more than stones. Let us take care, we who have left everything, lest for so small a thing we lose the kingdom of heaven. And if we ever find money we must pay no more attention to it than we do to the dust we tread on, because money is 'vanity of vanities, all is vanity' (see Eccles. 1:2). And if ever, which God forbid, a friar should pick up and appropriate money or coin, except in the above mentioned case of necessity for the sick, let all the friars regard him as a false brother, as a thief and a robber, as a possessor of goods, until he does penance. Friars shall never collect or arrange any collections for a house or building and they shall never accompany any people who beg in this way. All other offices not contrary to the Rule the friars may undertake with the blessing of God. Nevertheless, friars may beg alms for lepers in cases of absolute necessity. But they must fear money greatly. Likewise, all friars must shun searching the world for filthy gain.

### 9 Asking for alms

Let all the friars study to follow the humility and poverty of our Lord Jesus Christ. Let them remember that we must have nothing else in the world except, as the apostle Paul says, food and wherewith to be covered, and with these be content (see 1 Tim. 6:8). Let friars rejoice to be found in the company of lowly and despised people, the poor and weak, the sick and leprous and the beggars on the road. When it is necessary let them beg for alms on their behalf. Let them not imagine that this is shameful. Rather let them remember that our Lord Jesus Christ, the Son of the living and all powerful God, played the part of 'a most hard rock' (Isa. 50:7) and was not ashamed. Christ himself, his disciples and the virgin Mary lived on alms. When men humiliate the friars and refuse to give them alms, let them thank God for this. Through this shame they shall receive great honour at the judgement of our Lord Jesus Christ.

Let the friars remember that this humiliation will be imputed not to those who receive it but to those who cause it. Alms are a right and heritage due to the poor which have been won for us by our Lord Jesus Christ. Friars who receive the necessities of life through their work will be greatly rewarded. They will be the source of blessing to those who have been charitable towards them. Everything that men leave in the world shall perish. The only thing that remains is the charity and almsgiving they have done for which the Lord will recompense them.

Let the brothers tell each other what their needs are so that they can seek and receive what is necessary. Let each one love and nourish his brother as a mother loves and nourishes her child. God will give them grace for this. 'Let not him that eateth, despise him that eateth not: and he that eateth not, let him not judge him that eateth' (Rom. 14:3). Whenever the necessity arises all the friars, wherever they are, are allowed to eat the same food as other people eat. This is the same teaching that our Lord gave when he spoke of David eating the loaves that had been set aside for only the priests to eat (see Mark 2:26). Let the friars remember the word of the Lord, 'Take heed to yourselves, lest perhaps your hearts be overcharged with surfeiting and drunkenness and the cares of this life, and that day come upon you suddenly. For as a snare shall it come upon all that dwell upon the face of the earth' (Luke 21:34–35). Likewise, in times of obvious need let the brothers make what they lack as God directs them, for necessity has no law.

## 10 Sick friars
If, wherever he may be, one of the friars should become ill, the other friars are not to leave him, without at least one of them to tend him in the way they themselves would like to be looked after. However, in cases of absolute necessity, the ill friar may be left in the care of another person. I recommend that the sick friar should give thanks to the Creator for everything. If we are in good health or in bad health it is the will of the Lord. God teaches everyone he has predestined to eternal life through difficulties, sickness, trials and the grace of contrition. As the Lord himself said, 'Such as I love, I rebuke and chastise' (Rev.

3:19). The sick person should not complain or grumble against God or the friars or be over-anxious about his medicines or having his health restored, for his body will soon die and it is the enemy of the soul. If a friar acts like this he is being prompted by evil and by the flesh and he is unworthy of being numbered with the friars since he loves his body more than his soul.

## 11 The friars must not swear or slander, but love one another

The friars must take care not to slander anyone or be contentious. Rather they should keep silent for as long as God gives them grace. They must not argue among themselves or with other people. Rather let them regularly reply with humility, 'We are unprofitable servants' (Luke 17:10).

Let them not be angry, for 'Whosoever is angry with his brother, shall be in danger of the judgement. And whosoever shall say to his brother, Raca, shall be in danger of the council. And whosoever shall say, Thou fool, shall be in danger of hell fire' (Matt. 5:22). Let them love one another as the Lord commands, 'This is my commandment, that you love one another, as I have loved you' (John 15:12). Let them demonstrate through their deeds the love they should feel, as the apostle says: 'Let us not love in word, nor in tongue, but in deed, and in truth' (1 John 3:18). Let them speak evil about nobody and let them not murmur or slander, for it is written, 'Whisperers, detractors,' are 'hateful to God' (Rom. 1:29–30). Let them be gentle, 'shewing all mildness towards all men' (Titus 3:2). Let them not judge and condemn. As the Lord says, 'cast out first the beam out of thy own eye; and then shalt thou see to cast out the mote out of thy brother's eye' (Matt. 7:5). Let them strive to enter through the narrow gate, for the Lord says, 'Narrow is the gate, and strait is the way that leadeth to life; and few there are that find it!' (Matt. 7:14).

## 12 Guilty looks and avoiding women's company

All friars must, wherever they are or travel to, avoid evil glances from women and the company of women. No friar should talk alone with a woman. Priests should counsel women in a suitable way when they come for confession and spiritual advice. No woman should on any account make a vow of obedience to any friar. Once spiritual counsel has been given to her she should do penance wherever she wishes. We must all take care to stay pure in our minds, as the Lord says, 'Whosoever shall look on a woman to lust after her, hath already committed adultery with her in his heart' (Matt. 5:28).

## 13 Punishment for fornicators

If a friar, at the instigation of the devil, commits fornication, let him be deprived of the habit of the Order which he no longer has any right to because of his shameful behaviour. The friar must be completely cut off from his Order. Then he must do penance for his sins.

## 14 How the friars must travel through the world

When the friars travel through the world they must not carry anything with them, 'neither staff, nor scrip, nor bread, nor money' (Luke 9:3); and 'whatsoever house' they enter let them 'first say, "Peace be to this house"' (Luke 10:5–6). During their stay in the same house let them eat and drink what is set before them. Let them not resist evil, but if they are struck on the right cheek, let them turn the other also; and if their clothing and tunic are taken away, let them not resist. Let them give to all who ask. If what belongs to them is taken away, let them not reclaim it (see Matt. 5:39; Luke 6:29–30).

## 15 Friars must not own any animals or ride animals

I forbid all my friars, clerks and lay people, who go about the world or remain in their dwelling, to possess any animal either in their own or other people's houses, or in any other manner. And they are not allowed to ride on horseback except because of illness or any great necessity.

*16 Those to travel among Saracens and other unbelievers*
The Lord says, 'Behold I send you as sheep in the midst of wolves. Be ye therefore wise as serpents and simple as doves' (Matt. 10:16). Therefore all those friars who, through divine inspiration, wish to work among Saracens and other unbelievers, may do so with the permission of their minister and servant. And let the minister allow them and not refuse them, so long as he considers that they are suitable people to go. If he were to act imprudently in this matter, or in any other matter, he would have to give an account to the Lord.

There are two ways in which friars who live in this way should act. First, they are never to quarrel or argue, but be 'subject to every human creature for God's sake' (1 Pet. 2:13), while at the same time confessing themselves to be Christians. Second, when they think it will please God they are to herald the Word of God and to preach the faith of the almighty God, Father, Son and Holy Spirit. They are to preach about the universal Creator, the saving and redeeming Son, about being baptised into the Christian faith, for, 'unless a man be born again of water and the Holy Ghost, he cannot enter into the kingdom of God' (John 3:5).

These thoughts, with all others which God delights in, are the ones to be proclaimed to people. For the Lord says in the Gospels, 'Every one, therefore, that shall confess me before men, I will also confess him before my Father who is in heaven' (Matt. 10:32), and, 'he that shall be ashamed of me and of my words, of him the Son of Man shall be ashamed, when he shall come in his majesty, and that of his Father, and of the holy angels' (Luke 9:26).

All the friars everywhere must remember that they have given and handed themselves over body and soul to our Lord Jesus Christ. Out of love of him they must expose themselves to all visible and invisible enemies. For the Lord says, 'He that shall lose his life for my sake, shall save it' (Luke 9:24); 'Blessed are they that suffer persecution for justice' sake, for theirs is the kingdom of heaven' (Matt. 5:10); 'If they have persecuted me, they will also persecute you' (John 15:20); 'And when they shall persecute you in this city, flee into another' (Matt. 10:23); 'Blessed are ye when they shall revile you, and persecute you, and when they shall separate you, and shall reproach you, and cast out your name as evil and speak all that is evil against you, untruly, for my sake: Be glad in that day and rejoice, for your reward is very great in heaven' (Matt. 5:11–12 with Luke 6:22–23); 'I say unto you, my friends: Be not afraid of them who kill the body and after that have no more that they can do' (Luke 12:4); 'See that ye be not troubled' (Matt. 24:6); 'He that shall persevere unto the end, he shall be saved' (Matt. 10:22).

## 17 Preachers
[This is the little discourse given by St Francis to his friars departing for the first time to preach: 'Go, my well-beloved, two by two, into different parts of the world; preach peace and penitence to men for the remission of sins. Be calm and patient in the midst of your trials, for the Lord will fulfil his designs and promises. To those who question you reply humbly; bless those who persecute you; give thanks to those who revile and accuse you, for all that prepares for us an eternal kingdom.']

The friars must not preach contrary to the form and rules of the holy Roman Church, nor without the permission of his minister. Let the minister be careful not to grant it indiscreetly to anyone. But let all the friars preach according to their example. Let no minister or preacher claim for himself as a right the administration of the friars or the office of preaching. If he is ever ordered to leave those in his charge he must obey without question. In God's love I ask all my preaching friars, prayers and workers, ministers and lay people to be diligent in being humble in everything. They are not to boast or be puffed up with eloquent words or good deeds or about anything that God has done for them in their lives. For the Lord says, 'Rejoice not in this, that spirits are subject unto you; but rejoice in this, that your names are written in heaven' (Luke 10:20).

We must be certain that we possess nothing ourselves except for our sins and vices. We have good reason to rejoice when we are exposed to different temptations and when we suffer all kinds of tribulations and anguish of body and soul in this world, so that we can enter into eternal life. Also, my brothers, we must guard against all kinds of pride and vanity. Beware of the wisdom of this world and of the enticement of the flesh. The spirit of the flesh has little time for actions and is content with talk. It does not concentrate on religion and the inner holiness of the mind because it prefers a religion and saintliness of outward appearance. About such people the Saviour said, 'Amen I say to you, they have received their reward' (Matt. 6:2). The spirit of the Lord wills that the flesh is put to death, scorned, reviled, despised and abased. The spirit of the Lord seeks humility, patience, pure simplicity, true peace of mind and above everything else holy reverence, divine wisdom and love of the Father, the Son and the Holy Spirit.

We must ascribe all these good things to our sovereign Lord and most high God. We must acknowledge that all good belongs to him. We must thank him as all good things come from him. Let the sovereign most high Lord, the only true God, possess, receive and accept all honour and reverence, all praise and blessing, all acts of gratitude, all glory, since he alone is good and from him comes all goodness. When we observe any evil acts or hear God blasphemed, let us praise the Lord, let us do a good work and magnify him who is blessed for ever. Amen.

## 18 Ministers must meet together

Every year, on St Michael the Archangel's feast day, the

ministers must assemble with their brothers, wherever it is convenient for them, and talk together about the things of God. Every three years all the ministers who have gone over the seas or over the mountains shall come to the Chapter in the church of Santa Maria della Portiuncula, unless the minister and servant of the whole fraternity orders otherwise. Other ministers who have not travelled to distant lands shall do this annually.

## 19 Friars must live as Catholics

All the brothers must be Catholics and live and speak as Catholics. Anybody who sins through his speech or deeds against the Catholic faith and life, and who does not repent, is to be thrown out of the fraternity. In everything that concerns the salvation of the soul and is not against our religion, we are to look to all ministers as our masters and we are to venerate their order, office and conduct as if it came from God.

## 20 The friars' confessions and receiving the body and blood of our Lord Jesus Christ

Let my blessed friars, ordained and lay people, confess their sins to the priests of our Order. If they are not able to do this, let them confess to some other Catholic and prudent priest. They must know for certain that whichever priest they receive penance and absolution from they are definitely released from their sins, so long as they have faithfully and humbly performed the penance imposed on them. But if they cannot find a priest, let them confess to their brother, for the apostle James says, 'Confess therefore your sins one to another' (Jas. 5:16). In this case they must not forget to go afterwards to the priests who alone have power to bind and set free. Once they are contrite and have confessed their sins let them receive the body and blood of our Lord Jesus Christ with great humility and reverence. They must remember the word of the Lord, 'He that eateth my flesh, and drinketh my blood, hath everlasting life' (John 6:55); and also, 'Do this for a commemoration of me' (Luke 22:19).

## 21 Discourses and exhortations friars may give

All my friars shall, when it pleases them, give this discourse and exhortation, or a similar one before any audience, with God's blessing. 'Fear and honour, praise and bless, thank and adore the Lord God Almighty, in trinity and unity, Father, Son and Holy Spirit, the Creator of all. "Do penance: bring forth fruit worthy of penance, for you know that you must soon die" (see Matt. 3:2, 8; Luke 3:8–9). "Give, and it shall be given to you; forgive, and you shall be forgiven" (Luke 6:38, 37). If you do not forgive other people their sins the Lord will not forgive you your sins. Confess all your sins. Blessed are those who die penitent for they will enter the kingdom of heaven. Woe to those who do not die penitent for they will be sons of the devil whose deeds they do. They will go to the eternal fire. Be watchful and avoid all evil and persevere in good to the end.'

## 22 Exhortation to the friars

Let us all, my brothers, consider this word of the Lord, 'Love your enemies: do good to them that hate you' (Matt. 5:44). For our Lord Jesus Christ, in whose footsteps we must follow, gave the title of friend to a traitor, and he offered himself willingly to his executioners. People who unjustly bring on us troubles, afflictions, humiliations, insults, griefs, torments, martyrdom and death are our friends. We should love them even more than we love other people as they are instrumental in our attaining eternal life.

Let us hate our body with its vices and sins, because if we live for our bodies we shall lose the love of our Lord Jesus Christ and eternal life. We and all who belong to us will go to hell. Our sins make us vile and miserable. They oppose good and draw us to evil, because, as the Lord says in the Gospel, from the heart of man come forth evil thoughts, adulteries, fornications, murders, thefts, covetousness, wickedness, deceit, lasciviousness, an evil eye, false testimonies, blasphemies, pride and foolishness (see Matt. 15:19; Mark 7:21–22). All these evils come from within the heart of man and they defile the soul.

Now that we have renounced the world we have one more thing to do. We must be determined to follow the desire and will of the Lord. We must take care not to be like the stony and thorny ground by the wayside. According to the word of the Lord in the Gospel, 'The seed is the word of God' (Luke 8:11). The seed which fell by the wayside and was trodden down represents those who hear the word of God and do not understand it. Immediately the devil comes, takes possession of what was sown in their heart and takes away the word of God, lest believing they should be saved. As for that which falls upon the rock, it represents those who hear the word of God and at once receive it with joy. But as soon as tribulation or persecution comes they are offended by this word since they are not rooted in good soil. They believe for a time but when temptation comes they fall away. Some of the seed fell among thorns. This represents those who listen to the word of God, but the cares and worries of the world, the deceitfulness of riches choke the word and prevent it from bearing fruit. Finally the seed which falls on good ground describes those who have an undivided and good heart who bear fruit with patience (see Matt. 13:19–23; Mark 4:15–20; Luke 8:4–15).

That is why, my brothers, we should do as the Lord says, and 'let the dead bury their dead' (Matt. 8:22). We must be on guard against the malice and trickery of Satan. For Satan does not wish man to turn his heart and mind towards the Lord God. He prowls around and looks out for some way in which he can trap the human heart. He seeks to stifle the divine word in the human heart and to make it forget the Lord's commandments. Satan seeks to blind the heart with the cares and activities of the world so that he can live there instead. As the Lord says, 'When an unclean spirit has gone out of a man he walketh through dry places seeking rest, and findeth none. Then he saith: I will return into my house from whence I came out. And coming he findeth it empty, swept, and garnished. Then he goeth, and taketh with him seven other spirits more wicked than himself, and they enter in and dwell there: and the last state of that man is worse than the first' (Matt. 12:43–45).

So let us all, brothers, watch well over ourselves, in case the desire for a reward or a pleasure should make us lose everything and turn our mind and heart away from God. In the name of holy love, who is God, I implore all my brothers, ministers and others to lay aside every obstacle, every care, every trouble. We must serve, love, adore and honour the Lord with all our might, with a pure heart and with a healthy mind which God looks for above everything else. We must become a temple for the Lord God almighty, Father, Son and Holy Spirit, who has said, 'Watch ye, therefore, praying at all times, that you may be accounted worthy to escape all these things that are to come, and to stand before the Son of man' (Luke 21:36).

And when you pray, say, 'Our Father, who art in heaven' (Matt. 6:9). We must worship him with a pure heart, for 'we ought always to pray, and not to faint' (Luke 18:1). Those are the worshippers who seek the heavenly Father. 'God is a spirit, and they that adore him, must adore him in spirit and in truth' (John 4:24). Let us turn to him who is the shepherd and bishop of our souls. He says, 'I am the good shepherd,' I feed my sheep and 'give my life for the sheep' (see John 10:11). 'All you are brethren. Call none your father upon earth; for one is your Father, who is in heaven' (Matt. 23:9). Do not allow yourself to be called master, for Christ is your Master, who is in heaven (see Matt. 23:8–10). 'If you abide in me, and my words abide in you, you shall ask whatever you

will, and it shall be done unto you' (John 15:7). 'Where
there are two or three gathered together in my name,
there am I in the midst of them' (Matt. 18:20). 'Behold I
am with you all days, even to the consummation of the
world' (Matt. 28:20). 'The words that I have spoken to
you, are spirit and life' (John 6:64). 'I am the way, and the
truth, and the life' (John 14:6).

We must, therefore, hold fast the words, the life, the
doctrines of the holy gospel of him who deigned to pray to
his Father for us and to manifest his name in these words:

> *I have manifested thy name to the men whom thou hast*
> *given me . . . Because the words which thou gavest me, I*
> *have given to them; and they have received them, and*
> *have known in very deed that I came out from thee, and*
> *they have believed that thou didst send me. I pray for*
> *them: I pray not for the world, but for them whom thou*
> *hast given me: because they are thine: and all my things*
> *are thine. . . . Holy Father, keep them in thy name*
> *whom thou hast given me; that they may be one, as we*
> *also are. . . . These things I speak in the world, that they*
> *may have my joy filled in themselves. I have given them*
> *thy word, and the world hath given them thy word, and*
> *the world hath hated them, because they are not of the*
> *world, as I also am not of the world. I pray not that thou*
> *shouldst take them out of the world, but that thou*
> *shouldst keep them from evil. . . . Sanctify them in truth.*
> *Thy word is truth. As thou hast sent me into the world, I*
> *also have sent them into the world. And for them do I*
> *sanctify myself, that they also may be sanctified in truth.*
> *And not for them only do I pray, but for them also who*
> *through their word shall believe in me; that they all may*
> *be one . . . that the world may believe that thou hast sent*
> *me . . . and hast loved them, as thou hast also loved me.*
> *. . . And I have made known thy name to them . . . that*
> *the love wherewith thou hast loved me, may be in them,*
> *and I in them. Father, I will that where I am, they also*

*whom thou hast given me may be with me; and that they
may see my glory which thou hast given me (John 17:6–
26, 24).*

## 23 Prayer, praise and acts of grace

Sovereign God Almighty, most high, most holy, most
powerful, holy and just Father, Lord, king of heaven and
earth, we give thanks to thee for thyself. By thy will, by
thy only Son and by thy Holy Spirit, thou hast created
spiritual and corporal beings. Thou hast made us in thine
image and in thy likeness and placed us in paradise, which
through our fault we have lost. We give thanks to thee that
thou hast created us through thy Son, and that because of
the holy and true love with which thou hast loved us, thou
hast caused him to be born of the glorious and ever-
blessed virgin Mary, true man and true God. Thou hast
willed to redeem us from our captivity by his cross, his
death and his blood. We give thanks to thee because thy
Son himself will come in the glory of his majesty to drive
away into eternal fire the cursed who have not repented,
and have not known thee, and to say to those who have
known, adored and served thee with a contrite heart,
'Come, ye blessed of my Father, possess you the kingdom
prepared for you from the foundation of the world' (Matt.
25:34).

And because we all, miserable sinners, are not worthy
to call thee by thy name, we humbly pray that our Lord
Jesus Christ, thy well-beloved Son in whom thou art well
pleased, may give thee thanks with the Holy Spirit, the
Comforter, for all thy blessings, in a way acceptable to
thee. Thy Son is all sufficient, through whom thou hast
granted us so many favours. Alleluia! And you, glorious
and ever-blessed Mary, Mother of God, virgin ever,
blessed Michael, Gabriel and Raphael, all the choirs of
happy spirits, seraphim, cherubim, thrones, dominions,
principalities, powers, virtues, angels and archangels, holy
John the Baptist, John the Evangelist, Peter and Paul,

blessed patriarchs, prophets, saints, innocents, apostles, evangelists, disciples, martyrs, confessors, virgins, blessed Elijah and Enoch, and you all holy ones, present, past and to come, we beg you humbly for the love of God. We give thanks to him, the sovereign God, living and eternal, to his very dear Son, our Saviour Jesus Christ, and to the Holy Spirit, Paraclete, world without end. Amen. Alleluia.

And all those who shall serve the Lord God in the holy Catholic and Apostolic Church, all ecclesiastics, priests, deacons, subdeacons, acolytes, exorcists, readers, doorkeepers, all clerks, all monks and nuns, young men and children, poor and miserable ones, kings, princes, workmen, peasants, servants, masters, virgins, married people, continent ones, laity, men, women, the smallest children, girls and boys, youths and maidens, old people, the strong, the weak, the lowly and the great, all nations, families, tribes, languages and peoples, all men who are or shall be on the earth, we pray them humbly pray. We implore them, we, all unprofitable servants, to ask for us the grace of perseverance in true faith and penitence, for no one can be saved otherwise.

Let us all with all our heart, with all our soul, with all our mind, with all our strength, with all our efforts, with all our intelligence, with all our means, with all our inward parts, with all our desires, with all our whole will, love the Lord God, who has given and gives us all our bodies, our souls, our whole life, who has created us, redeemed us and saved us by his mercy alone, who has given and gives us all our blessings, us, miserable and unhappy, corrupted and vile, ungrateful and wicked.

Let us then have but one desire and one will, one pleasure and one delight. We must love and enjoy only our Creator, our Redeemer and our Saviour, and only true God, perfect and entire, lacking nothing, true and supreme, the only One who is alone mild and full of compassion, full of tenderness and sweetness, who alone is holy, just, good and true; who alone is all innocence and purity; from whom, in whom and by whom comes all pardon, grace, glory to all penitents, to all the just and blessed ones who rejoice in heaven. Let nothing turn us aside from that, let nothing separate, let nothing isolate us.

In every land, in every place, at all times, every moment, every day, continually, let us all trust truly and humbly from the bottom of our heart, let us love, honour, adore, serve, praise and bless, glorify, exalt, magnify and thank the most high, sovereign God, eternal Trinity in unity, Father, Son and Holy Spirit, Creator of all, Saviour of those who believe, trust and set their love on him, the unchanging God, without end and without beginning, invisible, unspeakable, ineffable, incomprehensible, unfathomable, blessed, praised, glorious, exalted, great, sublime, mild, compassionate, full of delight, entirely and above all things to be desired throughout all ages.

In the name of the Lord I beg all the friars to learn the text and sense of these words written in this Rule of life for the salvation of our souls. Let them frequently recall them to memory. And I pray the all-powerful God himself, three in one, to bless all those who shall teach, learn, possess, retain and put it into practice, each time that they shall repeat it and observe what is here written for our salvation. I pray them all, kissing their feet, to love, observe and keep this Rule. And on the part of almighty God, of the lord pope, and of obedience, I, Brother Francis, strictly command that no one shall take away from nor add to this written Rule, and that the friars shall not adopt any other.

Glory be to the Father, and to the Son, and to the Holy Spirit. As it was in the beginning, is now, and ever shall be, world without end. Amen.

## The Rule of the Friars Minor, 1223

*1 In the name of the Lord begins the life of the Friars Minor*
The Rule and life of the Friars Minor is this: to know how
to follow the holy gospel of our Lord Jesus Christ, living in
obedience, without possessions and in chastity. Brother
Francis promises obedience and reverence to the Lord
Pope Honorius, to his successors canonically elected and
to the Roman Church. And let the other friars be bound
to obey Brother Francis and his successors.

*2 Those who wish to embrace this life and how they should
be received*
If any wish to embrace this life and come to our friars,
they must go to their provincial ministers. These ministers, and nobody else, have the power to receive the
brothers. These ministers must question them carefully
about the Catholic faith and the church's sacraments.
They must believe all these things and live their lives in
accordance with them. They must be unmarried, or else
they and their wives must have taken the vow of conti-
nence and have received the permission of the diocesan
bishop. Or if their wives are so old that they are beyond
suspicion the minister will say to them, in the words of the
holy gospel, 'Go, sell whatsoever thou hast, and give to
the poor' (Mark 10:21). But if this cannot happen their
intention to do this is enough. The brothers and their
ministers must be aware about being anxious about
worldly possessions. Then they will be free to do what the
Lord suggests to them.

However, if advice is necessary, the ministers may then
send them to some God-fearing men who shall advise
them about how their goods may be distributed to the
poor. Once this has taken place they may receive the habit
of probation. This consists of two hoodless tunics, the
cord, the breeches and the chaperon reaching to the cord,
unless the ministers judge differently what is God's will.

When the probationary year is over they are received into obedience and promise always to obey this life and this Rule. They are never allowed to leave this Order, according to the lord pope's command, because the holy Gospel says, 'No man putting his hand to the plough, and looking back, is fit for the kingdom of God' (Luke 9:62).

Those who have already promised obedience may have a hoodless cloak as well as a hooded cloak. Those who find it necessary are allowed to wear shoes. All friars must wear cheap clothes. They can patch them with material from sacks and other pieces of cloth with God's blessing. I exhort and warn them against despising and condemning people they see who are dressed in fine and splendid clothes and who are used to eating and drinking delicacies. Instead the brothers are to judge and despise themselves.

### 3 The divine office, fasting and how friars should go about the world

Let the clerks recite the divine office according to the custom of the holy Roman Church, except for the Psalter, as soon as they can obtain breviaries. Let the lay brothers say twenty-four pater nosters for Matins, five for Lauds, seven for each of the following hours, Prime, Terce, Sext and None, twelve for Vespers, seven for Compline, and let them pray for the dead.

They must fast from the feast of All Saints to our Lord's nativity. Holy Lent begins at the Epiphany and lasts for forty days and is consecrated by our Lord's holy fast. Those who observe Lent voluntarily will be blessed by the Lord and those who do not wish to observe Lent should not be forced to. They should only be bound to fast on Fridays. However, friars should not be compelled to fast when it is absolutely impossible for them to do so.

I counsel, warn and exhort my brothers in the Lord Jesus Christ that when they go into the world they should avoid all disputes and worldly discussions. They should not judge other people but be gentle, peaceful, modest, full of meekness and humility, speaking honestly to everyone, as is appropriate.

They are not allowed to ride on horseback unless necessity or illness dictates. 'Into whatsoever house you enter, first say: Peace to this house' (Luke 10:5). As it is stated in the holy Gospel they are allowed to eat whatever food is set before them.

### 4 Friars must not accept money

I strictly command all the friars never to receive coin or money for themselves or on behalf of anyone else. However, for the necessities of the sick and for clothing for other friars, the ministers and guardians must, with the help of spiritual friends, be most careful to supply what is necessary according to places and time and cold climates. As has already been stated, they are not to receive coin or money.

### 5 Working

Let the friars to whom the Lord has given the grace to work do so faithfully and devoutly. They should work so that they expel idleness, the enemy of the soul, but do not extinguish the spirit of holy prayer and devotion, to which all other temporal things should be subject. As far as payment for work is concerned they are allowed to receive for themselves and their brothers the necessities for the body, but they are not allowed to receive coins and money. They are to live with the kind of humility that is appropriate to God's servants and the disciples of most holy poverty.

### 6 The friars are to appropriate nothing. Asking alms for themselves and for sick friars

The friars are not allowed to appropriate houses or anything else. They are to go about confidently asking for alms since they are strangers and pilgrims on the earth, serving the Lord in humility and poverty. They should not be embarrassed to do this since the Lord made himself poor in this world for our sakes. This is where the virtue of poverty lies. Poverty has made you, my very dear brothers, heirs and kings in the kingdom of heaven. You are poor in earthly possessions but rich in virtue. Let poverty be your heritage and lead you to the land of the living. Completely attach yourselves to poverty, much loved brothers, and in the name of our Lord Jesus Christ never desire to possess anything under heaven.

Wherever the friars meet each other let there be mutual service. With confidence they are to share their needs with each other. For if a mother loves and cares for her child according to the flesh, how much more affectionately should each friar love and care for his brother according to the spirit. If a friar should become ill let the other friars care for him in the way that they would like to be cared for.

## 7 The penance to be imposed on friars who have fallen into sin

If any friars commit mortal sin, at the instigation of the enemy, and have been instructed to go to the provincial ministers, the friars should do so without any delay. But let the ministers, if they are priests, impose penance on them mercifully. If they are not priests themselves the penance shall be imposed by other priests of the Order, as seems appropriate to them in the Lord. They must avoid being annoyed and troubled by the sin of any friar as anger stifles charity in oneself and in others.

## 8 The election of the minister-general to this fraternity. The Chapter at Pentecost

All the friars must have one of the members of the fraternity over them as minister-general and servant of the whole fraternity. Friars are bound to obey him absolutely. On the death of the minister-general, the election of a successor must be made by the provincial ministers and the guardians at the Whitsun Chapter. The provincial ministers must attend this meeting at whatever place the minister-general has selected. Every three years, or more frequently, or less frequently, the minister-general will organise such meetings. If the majority of the provincial ministers and guardians should think the minister-general unsuitable to serve the common good of the friars, these same ministers and guardians must, in the name of the Lord, elect another as guardian. After the Whitsun Chapter, if the ministers and guardians think it appropriate, they may assemble a Chapter of the friars in their custodies once in the same year.

## 9 Preachers

The friars must not preach in any diocese where the bishop objects to them preaching. The friar must not preach to the people if he has not been examined and approved by the minister-general of this fraternity and received permission from him to preach. I also warn and exhort my friars that in their preaching they must select their words carefully. They should preach for the benefit and instruction of the people. They should preach about vices as well as virtues, misery as well as glory, in short addresses, because the Lord made his word short upon earth (Rom. 9:28).

## 10 The admonition and correction of friars

Let the friars who are ministers and servants of the other friars visit and admonish their friars. They must correct them humbly and lovingly and should never order them to do anything that is against their conscience or our Rule. But let the friars who are being corrected remember that they have given up their own will for God's sake. I command them to obey carefully their ministers in everything which they have vowed to the Lord to observe and which is not against their souls and our Rule. Wherever there may be friars who find it impossible to obey the Rule completely they are to visit their ministers. These ministers must receive these friars with charity and kindness and be so open to them that these friars can speak and act with them as masters with their servants. This is how it should be since the ministers are the servants of all the friars.

In addition to this, I give this warning to the friars. I exhort them in the Lord Jesus Christ to keep themselves from all pride, vainglory, envy, avarice, cares and anxieties of this world, from detraction and murmuring. Those who are unable to read should not be forced to learn to read. Above everything else they should desire to possess the spirit of the Lord and his holy deeds. They should pray to God with a pure heart, be humble and patient in persecution and illness. They should love those who persecute us, reprove and blame us, for the Lord says, 'Love your enemies . . . pray for them that persecute and calumniate you' (Matt. 5:44). 'Blessed are they that suffer persecution for justice' sake: for theirs is the kingdom of heaven' (Matt. 5:10). 'He that shall persevere unto the end, he shall be saved' (Matt. 10:22).

*11 The friars must not enter convents of nuns*
I strictly command all the friars to have no dealings or suspicious talks with women and not to enter into nuns' convents, unless they have received special permission from the apostolic see. They must not be godfathers to any men or women, in case this causes a scandal among the friars or in case a scandal is caused by the friars.

*12 Those who go among the Saracens or other unbelievers*
All friars who wish to go among the Saracens and other unbelievers must ask the permission of their provincial ministers. The ministers should only grant this permission to the people who seem suitable to be sent.

I also order ministers, for the sake of being obedient, to ask the lord pope to grant that one of the cardinals of the holy Roman Church may be governor, protector and superior of this fraternity. In this way we will always be obedient and submissive to the feet of this holy church, and strong in the catholic faith, so that we may observe the poverty and humility and the holy gospel of our Lord Jesus Christ, which we have firmly promised.

## The Rule of the Order of Penitents, or of the Third Order

Here begins the Rule and the Life of the Brothers and Sisters of Penitence. Amen.

In the name of the Father, and of the Son and of the Holy Spirit. Amen.

### 1 Dress

The men who belong to this fraternity should dress in poor clothes which must not be brightly coloured. The cloth they wear should be wide and thick and their clothing is to be fastened near the neck, but not with brooches. They are not to dress like worldly people and they must not have wide sleeves.

The sisters' clothing and tunics should be made of similar materials to the brothers' clothing. In addition to their habits they should at least have a petticoat or another garment. It can be black or white and it can be an ample linen cloak without folds. They are not allowed to wear scarves or silk ribbons. The brothers and sisters are allowed to wear lambswool but no other furs. They may have leather purses and belts but they must not be embroidered in silk. They must not attend banquets or plays or dances. They and their families are not allowed to befriend actors.

### 2 Abstinence

Everyone must abstain from eating meat except on Sundays, Tuesdays and Thursdays. Illness or tiredness from travelling are exceptions to this rule. You need not fast on major festival days. Such major festivals include our Lord's nativity, the first two days of the new year, Epiphany, Easter and the two days after Easter, St Peter's day, St Paul's day, the nativity of John the Baptist, the assumption of the glorious virgin Mary, the feast of All Saints and St Martin's day. On the days when you are not fasting you are allowed to eat cheese and eggs. People living in convents may eat what is set before them. Everyone, except for the weak, the ill and those who have travelled should be content with dinner and supper. Those who are in good health should eat and drink with moderation. They should say the 'Our Father' before and after the midday and evening meals. Let them give thanks to the Lord. At other meals they are to say 'Our Father' three times.

## 3 Fasting

They are to fast on Fridays from Easter to All Saints day. From All Saints day to Easter they are to fast on Wednesdays as well as Fridays. They must observe other fasts which the whole church prescribes. All through St Martin's Lent, from the day after Christmas, they must fast. They must fast during the great Lent, from Quinquagesima until Easter, unless illness or some other reason prevents them. Pregnant sisters may be excused from bodily mortifications until their churching, except with regard to dress and prayings. People engaged in manual labour are allowed to eat three meals a day from Easter to the dedication of St Michael. When they are engaged in work at other people's houses they may eat what is set before them, except on Fridays and other fast days which have been prescribed for everyone by the church.

## 4 Prayers

Every day everyone must recite the seven canonical hours,

that is to say Matins, Prime, Terce, Sext, None, Vespers and Compline. Those who know 'Lord have mercy on me' and 'I believe in God' should say them at Prime and Compline. If you are unable to say the office at the correct time you must at least say the Our Fathers. Ill people need not recite the hours unless they wish to.

### 5 Attendance at Matins
Everyone must attend Matins during the Lent of St Martin and the Great Lent, unless personal circumstances make it impossible.

### 6 Confession, communion, debts, bearing arms and taking oaths
You should go to confession three times a year, at our Lord's nativity, at Easter and at Pentecost.

Always pay the taxes you owe and the taxes that you will be charged in the future.

You are not to bear arms against anyone.

Abstain from taking a solemn oath unless you are forced to by a case of necessity and then only do so according to the sovereign pontiff's act of concession. You are only allowed to take a solemn oath for the sake of peace, faith, slander and giving evidence in court.

In your conversations you must avoid oaths as much as possible. If, through a slip of the tongue, you do thoughtlessly swear, as is often the case among the loquacious, you must examine your conscience that evening and say three Our Fathers.

You must all encourage your own family to serve God.

### 7 Mass and the monthly meeting
Each month the brothers and sisters of every town or area must meet together in a church that has been selected by the ministers. There you must assist in the worship and listen to the divine word. Each person should give a coin to the collector. The treasurer will

keep the money which will be distributed by the Council of Ministers to poor brothers and sisters, especially the sick and for funeral expenses for those who would not otherwise be able to afford a funeral. Part of the money should also be given to the poor and to the church where they meet.

If at all possible, you should have a friar who is instructed in the Word of God to speak to you and encourage you in penitence, perseverance and in carrying out deeds of mercy. You must remain silent during the mass and the sermon and pay careful attention as the office is read.

## 8 Illness

If a brother or sister becomes ill and sends word to a minister he should make weekly visits to the sick person. If he cannot go himself he must arrange for someone else to make these visits. The visitor should exhort the ill person to be penitent and give him what his body requires, using money from the common treasury.

## 9 Dead brothers

When a sick person dies tell the brothers and sisters of the town or place. They can then help with the burying of the body and not leave until the mass is finished.

During the week following the death the priest must say one mass, fifty psalms if he knows the Psalter and fifty Our Fathers with the *Requiem aeternam* ('Rest eternal') at the end of each for the soul of the deceased.

During the following year the priest is to say three masses, the priest who knows the Psalter is to say the Psalter, and the priests who do not know the Psalter are to say one hundred Our Fathers with the *Requiem aeternam* at the end of each for the salvation of the brothers and sisters who are alive or dead. If they forget to do this then they have to say twice as many Psalms or Our Fathers with the *Requiem aeternam*.

## 10 Making wills

People who are entitled to make wills should do so for they should not die intestate. They should dispose of their goods during the three months after they become monks. They should settle disputes between brothers, sisters and strangers. They should do what ministers see fit and consult with the diocesan bishop where he can assist. If the leading laymen of the places where the brothers and sisters live become upset over any of their rights and privileges the local ministers, on advice from the lord bishop, should do what they think is best.

Everyone must receive and faithfully fulfil the ministry and other offices which are set out here. Each person may be exempted from office for one year. When anyone enquires about entering the fraternity the ministers should find out about his circumstances and his work and explain to him the duties of the Order, with particular reference to the restitution of possessions. If the candidate finds the fraternity to his liking he should be given the habit and he should settle his debts by paying money or giving a security. He should be reconciled to his neighbour and he should pay his taxes. When this has happened, and after a year has elapsed, if it seems good to some prudent brothers, he should be received in the following manner. He must promise to observe everything that is written here as well as anything that may be added or taken away from this writing by the friars. He must do this for his whole life unless the ministers decide otherwise. If anyone disobeys this Order he is to be warned by the ministers and do the penance imposed by the visiting senior cleric. His promise to obey the order should be put in writing and made public. No one is to be received in any other way unless the ministers decide otherwise on account of the person's rank or because of the person's own request. No one should leave the fraternity or stray from these rules except to enter another religious order.

## 11 Heresy

No heretic or person suspected of heresy is to be admitted
to the fraternity. If the candidate is only suspected of heresy he should prove himself in front of the bishop before
being admitted. Married women may only be received
with the consent of their husbands. Incorrigible brothers
and sisters who have been expelled from the fraternity
must not be readmitted, except with the consent of the
most trustworthy of the friars.

## 12 Being accused of faults

The ministers of each town and place must inform the visitor of the brothers' and sisters' faults so that they may be
punished. Incorrigible brothers and sisters should be
denounced to the visitor by the minister once he has taken
advice from some discreet brothers. The incorrigible
brother or sister deserves to be expelled from the fraternity and this should be declared in front of the whole congregation. If this person should be a friar the local
authorities should also be informed.

If anyone is aware of a brother or a sister causing a scandal the minister should be informed and the visitor
warned, unless it is a problem between a husband and a
wife. The visitor, on his own discretion, has the power to
grant a dispensation to any brother or sister.

At the end of each year the ministers, having taken
advice from a friar, should appoint two more ministers
and a faithful treasurer to provide for the needs of the
brothers and sisters and other poor people. Deputies
should also be appointed who are to report on the conversations and actions of the fraternity.

## 13 Admitting faults

No brother should become a surety for anyone else unless
it is for a member of the fraternity and is with the permission of the visitor or the minister. In the same way the visitor may, with the consent of the ministers and other

friars, allow brothers to stay away from church for some time, provided that they say Matins and their other hours. Also, each brother must confess to a priest once a month as holy confession washes away all sins and gives divine grace more abundantly.

Each month the brothers should assemble for mass with the Friars Minor unless the visitor or minister has allowed them to stay away. On the same day they must assemble again after None. If a visitor or minister is unable to attend on this day they are to appoint a vicar to take his place so that the holy fraternity is not affected.

Any brother who has been involved in a scandal is to admit this before the monthly assembly of the brothers. If he fails to do this a brother should accuse him of his scandal. Then the visitor, minister or vicar will impose a penance unless the scandal requires him to be expelled from the Order.

No new rule is to be accepted unless the majority of the fraternity agree with it.

No brother is to take another brother to court without the consent of the visitor, minister and the majority of the members of the congregation. Where any dispute between brothers arises it should be settled by some discreet brothers. The brother who brings the complaint should bow to the decision of the visitor so that scandal may be avoided.

## Fragments of the Rule of the Sisters of St Clare

*The promise of St Francis to St Clare*
Through divine inspiration you have become daughters and servants of the most high celestial Father, the sovereign King. You have taken the Holy Spirit as a husband by choosing a life in accordance with the perfection of the holy gospel.

I and my friars wish and promise always to show diligent care and special solicitude for you as well as for them.

*The last wish St Francis wrote for St Clare*
I, little Brother Francis, wish to follow the life and poverty of the most high God, our Lord Jesus Christ, and his most holy mother and to persevere in this way to the end. And I beseech you, my ladies, and I counsel you to live always in this most holy life of poverty. Be on your guard against the influence of any strange teaching and advice so that you never deviate from your life of poverty in any way.

## Living in a Hermitage

Friars who desire to live together in hermitages should do so in threes, or, at the largest, in fours. Two of them should act as mothers and two of them should behave as children (or just one of them if there are only three of them). The first two should live like Martha and the other two like Mary Magdalene.

People living like Mary should have a cloister. They should each have their own cell, as they must not live or sleep together. They are to say Compline daily, at sunset. They must be strict about keeping silent. They must say all their services and get up for Matins. They must seek 'first the kingdom of God and his justice' (Luke 12:31). They must say Prime and Terce at the correct time. Once Terce is over they can break their silence and speak with their mothers. If they need to they are allowed to ask alms from them for the love of the Lord God, just as very poor people do. Later they must recite Sext, None and Vespers at the correct times.

No one is allowed to come into or eat in their cloisters. The friars who are acting as mothers must take care to avoid all strangers. As they obey their minister they must keep everyone away from their children and let no one speak to them. These children are only allowed to speak with their mothers. But they can speak with God's blessing to their guardian when he visits them. The children and the mothers are to change places in whatever way they care to arrange. Everyone must be diligent and faithful in observing this counsel.

# TESTAMENTS

## The Testament of St Francis

The Lord has given me, Brother Francis, grace to begin to do penance in the following way. When I was in sin I was very upset at the sight of lepers. But the Lord himself led me to them and then I cared for them. When I left them, what had previously seemed bitter to me was changed into sweetness of soul and body. After a short time I came out from this world. And the Lord gave me such great faith in the churches that I worshipped him with simplicity and said, 'We adore thee, Lord Jesus Christ, here and in all thy churches on this earth, and we bless thee for having redeemed the world by thy holy cross.'

Afterwards the Lord gave me, and still gives me, such great faith in the priests who live according to the rule of the holy Roman Church, because of their character, that, even if they persecute me, I shall have recourse to them. Even if I had all of Solomon's wisdom and I found some poor priests in this world, I would not preach against their will in their own parishes. I want to fear, love and honour these priests, and all other priests, as my lords. I will not find any sin in them since I look on them as being the sons of God and because they are my lords. I behave like this because in this world I do not see the body of the most high Son of God if it is not his most holy body and blood which the priests receive and which they alone minister to others. Above everything else I want these most holy mysteries to be honoured and revered and placed in precious holy places. As for the most holy name of the Lord, and for his written words, if I find them in any inappropriate places, I collect them and beg others to collect them and put them in an appropriate place. We must honour and venerate all theologians and people who spread the most holy divine words as people who communicate to us spirit and life.

When the Lord gave me friars, no human person showed me what to do, but the most high God revealed to me that I must live according to the rule of the holy gospel. I wrote this rule down using a few, simple words and the lord pope confirmed it. [One day while St Francis was weeping over his sins, he was consoled by the Lord and was granted a vision about the future of his Order: 'Have courage,' he said afterwards to his friars, 'and rejoice in the Lord; you are few in number, but do not be sad or dismayed at either my simplicity or your own simplicity. For the Lord has clearly shown me that God will make you into a large number and through his blessing you will grow and extend.'] The people who joined us gave all they could to the poor. They were content with one tunic, patched both on the inside and the outside, and with the cord and the breeches. And we wished for no more.

We clerks say the Office like other clerks, the lay brothers say the Lord's Prayer and have willingly remained in the churches. We are submissive to all. I worked with my hands, and continue to work like this, and urge all other friars to engage in honest work. Those who do not know how to work must learn to do so. They must not work hoping to be paid for their work but as a good example and to expel idleness. When we are not given payment for our work we go to the Lord's table and beg alms from door to door.

We must use this greeting which the Lord revealed to me: 'The Lord give thee peace.' The friars must not accept churches, poor dwellings, nor any other places built for them unless they conform to the poverty which is laid down in the Rule. We are to live here on earth as strangers and pilgrims.

I strictly forbid all my friars to request letters from the court of Rome either for themselves or for other people. They are not allowed to do this using preaching or the desire to avoid persecution as a pretext. Wherever they are not welcomed they are to move on and do penance with God's blessing. I firmly desire to obey the minister-general of this fraternity and the guardian he appoints over me. I want to be completely in his hands so that I cannot move or act against his wishes because he is my master. Although I am simple and weak I nevertheless wish always to have a clerk to recite the Office as set out in the Rule.

In the same way, all the other friars must obey their guardians and say the Office according to the Rule. This is the action you are to take against any friars who refuse to say this Office according to the Rule but wish to vary it in some way, or who are in some other way not catholic-minded. All the other friars, wherever they may be, must take these wayward friars to the nearest guardian. The guardian must confine him night and day as if he were in a prison. Nobody must be able to take this friar away until the guardian himself gives him back into the hands of the minister. The minister has no alternative but to send him, under the guard of some brothers who are to treat him like a prisoner day and night, to be presented to the lord of Ostia. For the lord of Ostia is master, protector and superior to the whole fraternity.

The friars must never say, 'This is another Rule'. This is a remembrance, a warning and an exhortation. This is my testament, that I, little Brother Francis, give to you, my blessed brothers so that you may observe the Rule we have promised to the Lord, in a more catholic way. The minister-general and all the other ministers and guardians are forbidden to add anything or to take anything away from these words. In the chapters they attend, when they read the Rule, let them also read these words. I strictly command all my friars, clerk and lay, to be obedient in this, and to put no glosses on the Rule or on these words, saying, 'They must be understood thus'. As the Lord has given me grace to say and write the Rule purely and simply in these words, you also must understand them purely and simply. You must always put them into practice with the help of God's holy grace.

May whoever observes these things be filled from heaven with the blessing of the most high celestial Father. On earth may they be filled with the blessing of his well-beloved Son, and the Holy Spirit, the Paraclete, and with all the powers of heaven and from all the saints. And I, Brother Francis, your little servant, as far as I am able, confirm this very holy benediction. So be it.

[On his death-bed St Francis gave this blessing to Brother Elias and to the Order:

I bless thee, son, in all and above all; and because in thy hands the most high God has increased my brothers and my children, over thee and in thee, I bless them all. From heaven and on earth may the sovereign Lord bless thee with all things. I bless thee as much as I can and more than I can; and what I cannot do from myself, may he who can do all things grant thee. May God be mindful of thy work, and of thy trouble, and may thy share be laid up at the recompense of the just. Mayst thou find all the blessings you desire and may your just demands be granted.

Farewell, all my children, in the fear of the Lord, always live in him, for there are great trials approaching you as tribulation approaches. Happy are those who persevere in the way in which they have begun. There will be scandals in the future which will separate some of you. As for me, I hasten towards my Lord and my God. I have devoutly served him from the depths of my soul. I go to him with confidence.]

**Testament written in April 1226**

Write that I bless all my brothers in religion and all who
shall become my brothers in religion. Since I am unable to
speak because of my weakness, my pain and my sickness, I
will express my desires and wishes for all the present
brothers and all the brothers in three words. In memory
and remembrance of my benediction and last will they
must always love each other as I have loved them and as I
still cherish them. They must always love and follow our
lady poverty. They must always faithfully obey the pre-
lates and clerics of our holy mother, the church.

# ADMONITIONS OF ST FRANCIS

## 1 The body of Christ

The Lord Jesus said to his disciples, 'I am the way, and the truth, and the life. No man cometh to the Father, but by me. If you had known me, you would without doubt have known my Father also: and from henceforth you shall know him, and you have seen him. Philip said to him: Lord, show us the Father, and it is enough for us. Jesus saith to him: Have I been so long a time with you, and have you not known me? Philip, he that seeth me seeth the Father also' (John 14:6–9). The Father 'inhabiteth light inaccessible' (1 Tim. 6:16), and 'God is spirit' (John 4:24), and 'no man hath seen God at any time' (John 1:18). Because God is spirit, spirit alone can see God; for it 'is the spirit that quickeneth: the flesh profiteth nothing' (John 6:63).

But the Son, in as much as he is equal to the Father, cannot be seen by anyone except the Father and the Holy Spirit. Thus all those who since our Lord Jesus Christ have seen humanity without seeing his spirit and his divinity and without believing that he is the true Son of God, were condemned. Likewise all those who see the sacrament of the body of Christ, consecrated by the words of the Lord on the altar in the hands of the priest under the appearance of bread and wine, and who do not see his spirit and his divinity and do not believe it to be truly the most holy body and blood of our Lord Jesus Christ, those also are condemned. The testimony of the almighty God himself says, 'This is my body' and 'the blood of the new testament' (see Mark 14:22–24), and, 'He that eateth my flesh and drinketh my blood hath everlasting life' (John 6:54).

So those who are faithful to God have the spirit of God dwelling in them. He receives the most holy body and blood of the Lord. Everybody else who has no part in this spirit and yet dares to communicate eat and drink judgement to themselves (see 1 Cor. 11:29). 'O ye sons of men, how long will you be hard of heart?' (Ps. 4:3). Why do you not know the truth and believe in the Son of God? Every day he humiliates himself just as he did when he left his royal throne and came to the womb of a virgin. Each day he comes to you in a humble way. Each day he comes down from the heart of his Father to the altar in the hands of the priest. Just as he showed himself to his apostles in his body, so he shows himself to us in the sacred bread. When they looked at Jesus' body they only observed his humanity, even though they believed in and contemplated his divinity. When we see the bread and wine with our human eyes we firmly believe that there are his most holy body and his true and living blood. This is how the Lord is always with his disciples, as he himself says, 'Behold, I am with you all days, even to the consummation of the world' (Matt. 28:20).

## 2 The vice of self-will

The Lord said to Adam, 'Of every tree of paradise thou shalt eat: but of the tree of knowledge of good and evil, thou shalt not eat' (Gen. 2:16–17). Adam then could eat of the fruit of every tree of paradise, and as long as he did nothing against obedience he did not sin. The person who eats from the tree of the knowledge of good regards his will as his own property and boasts about the good deeds which the Lord shows and works in him. He listens to the suggestions of the devil, breaks God's commands and so discovers the fruit of the knowledge of evil. He will have to bear the penalty for this.

## 3 Perfect and imperfect obedience

In the gospel, the Lord says, 'Every one of you that doth not renounce all that he possesseth, cannot be my disciple' (Luke 14:33), and 'He that will save his life, shall lose it' (Matt. 16:25). He abandons everything that he possesses, loses his body and his soul, and gives himself up entirely to obedience in the hands of his superior. All his actions, all his thoughts, provided they are good and not opposed to the will of his superior, are fruits of true obedience. Even if the subject should see things which are more profitable for his soul than the prelate commands, let him nevertheless surrender his will to God. His duty is to aim at accomplishing the orders of his prelate. That is true and charitable obedience, and pleasing to God and one's neighbour.

If a prelate gives a command which is against the conscience of someone under him, that person may disobey the prelate, but does not have to leave him. If this results in persecution the person under the prelate's command should love his superiors all the more for God's sake. The person who prefers persecution to separation from his brothers really dwells in the true spirit of obedience, since he is sacrificing his life for his brothers. There are many religious people who, with the excuse of knowing better than their superiors, 'look back' and return to the vomit of their own will (see Luke 9:62; Prov. 26:11). All these people are guilty of murder and their dire examples cause many souls to be lost.

## 4 No one shall take the appointment of superior on himself

'[I am] not come to be ministered unto, but to minister' (Matt. 20:28), says the Lord. Let those who are appointed to govern the others boast no more about their superiority than if they were ordered to wash their brothers' feet. They should be no more disturbed about losing the office of superior than they would if they lost the office of foot washing. If they are worried about losing the office of superior their soul's salvation is exposed to danger.

## 5 Let no one boast except in the Lord's cross

Consider what an excellent position the Lord has placed you in. He has created you, formed a body in the image of his well-beloved Son and a soul in his own likeness. All creatures on earth serve the Creator in their own way and they know and obey him more than you. The demons did not crucify him, for it was you who agreed with those who crucified him. Each time you delight in vice and sin you crucify him afresh. Are you able to boast about this? You might be clever and intelligent. You might possess all knowledge. You might be able to speak every language in the world and be able to search closely into celestial problems. None of that would give you reason to think well of yourself. A single demon has known more about heavenly things and earthly things than any person, even though some men have received special knowledge from God. You might be the richest and most beautiful person in the world. You might be able to perform miracles. You might be able to drive demons out of people. But all that would be of no advantage to you and you would not be able to boast about anything. However, we may boast in our infirmities and in the daily bearing of the holy cross of our Lord Jesus Christ.

# 6 Imitating our Lord

Let us all meditate, brothers, on the Good Shepherd who bore the suffering of the cross for the salvation of his sheep. The Lord's sheep have followed him in tribulation, in persecution, in shame, in hunger and in thirst, in weakness, in temptations and in other trials. For this faithfulness they have received eternal life from the Lord. Moreover, since we are God's servants, it is to our great shame that the saints have practised these virtues. We talk about them and preach that people should follow their example and for doing this we think we should receive glory and honour.

# 7 Good deeds should accompany knowledge

The apostle Paul says, 'The letter killeth, but the spirit quickeneth' (2 Cor. 3:6). The letter kills those people who only want to know the text so that they can appear to be wise in other people's eyes. They seek to acquire riches which they then give to their neighbours and friends. Religious people are also killed by the letter when they do not follow the spirit of holy books, but prefer to know them only by the words and interpret them to others.

On the other hand, the people who are quickened by the spirit of the holy scriptures do not interpret the text literally when they study and examine it. These people trace the word and example back to the Lord who is the source of all goodness.

# 8 Avoiding the sin of envy

The apostle Paul says, 'No man can say the Lord Jesus, but by the Holy Ghost' (1 Cor. 12:3). Whoever envies his brother because of the good things the Lord says to him

and does for him is almost committing the sin of blas-
phemy. He is envying the most high God himself who is
the source and author of all goodness.

## 9 Love

The Lord says in the Gospel, 'Love your enemies: do good
to them that hate you' (Matt. 5:44). The person who is not
hurt by the injuries received from an enemy is truly loving
him. You truly love your enemy when, for God's sake,
you grieve over your enemy's sin and when you
demonstrate your affection by your actions.

## 10 The mortification of the body

Many people blame their enemy or their neighbour when
they themselves sin or suffer an injury. It is quite wrong to
do this. For each person has his enemy, his body, through
which he sins. Happy is the servant who always keeps this
enemy chained up and wisely guards himself against evil
attacks. As long as he acts in this way no other enemy, visible or invisible, can hurt him.

## 11 Against letting oneself be influenced by an evil example

Nothing can be more displeasing to God's servant than
sin. In whatever way a person may sin, if God's servant
grieves and becomes angry about it he is storing up wrath
for himself, unless he is acting from love. ['Despisest thou
the riches of [God's] goodness, and patience, and long-
suffering? Knowest thou not that the benignity of God
leadeth thee to penance? But according to thy hardness
and impenitent heart, thou treasurest up to thyself wrath,

against the day of wrath, and revelation of the just judgment of God' (Rom. 2:4–5).] God's servant who worries and troubles himself about nothing leads an upright and faultless life. Blessed is he who keeps nothing for himself, rendering 'to Caesar the things that are Caesar's; and to God, the things that are God's' (Matt. 22:21).

## 12 The knowledge of the Spirit of the Lord

This is the way that you can recognise if the Lord's servant has the Spirit of God. When God does some good deed in him he will not be puffed up by it if he is living by the Spirit. But he will be opposed to it if he is living in the body. The Lord's servant has the spirit of the Lord if he sufficiently despises himself in his own eyes and if he considers himself inferior to all other people.

## 13 Patience

One cannot estimate how much interior patience and humility God's servant possesses while he is happy. But when those who should be friendly towards him are not, then he reveals how much patience and humility he really possesses.

## 14 Poverty of spirit

'Blessed are the poor in spirit: for theirs is the kingdom of heaven' (Matt. 5:3). Many people are faithful in praying and faithful at attending the divine Office, and practice abstinence and bodily mortification. But as soon as they suffer an injury or are deprived of something they are at once offended. This is not the way to be poor in spirit. For he who is truly poor in spirit hates himself and cherishes those who strike him on the cheek (see Matt. 5:35).

## 15 Peacemakers

'Blessed are the peacemakers: for they shall be called the
children of God' (Matt. 5:9). People who, in the middle of
all their sufferings, in the middle of the world, preserve
exterior and interior peace for the love of our Lord Jesus
Christ are truly peacemakers.

## 16 Purity of heart

'Blessed are the clean of heart: for they shall see God'
(Matt. 5:8). People who despise the world, seek heaven
and never cease to adore and to see with a pure heart and
mind the true and living God are the clean of heart.

## 17 The humble servant of God

Blessed is that servant who no more glories in the good
said and done in him by the Lord than in that said and
done in others. The man who exacts from his neighbour
more than he himself gives to the Lord his God sins.

## 18 Compassion towards one's neighbour

Happy is the person who bears his neighbour's infirmities
in the way that he himself would like to be treated.

## 19 The happy and the unhappy servant

Blessed is that servant who attributes all his goods to the
Lord his God. The person who retains anything for himself hides his Master's money, and what 'he thinketh he
hath, shall be taken away from him' (Luke 8:18).

## 20 The humble and good person

Blessed is that servant who does not look on himself as better when he is praised and exalted by men than when he is reckoned vile, simple and contemptible. Whatever a person is before God, that he is indeed and nothing more. Woe to the religious person who is set in a place of honour by his brothers and will never give it up. On the other hand, happy is the servant who does not take a superior place by his own efforts but who constantly desires to sit at the feet of other people.

## 21 The blessed and the foolish people

Blessed is the religious person who finds his pleasure and joy in holy discourse and in the deeds of the Lord. This person is blessed when he uses these means to lead men to the love of God with joy and gladness. But woe to the religious people who delight in vain and idle words and who therefore give people reason to mock.

## 22 Frivolous and talkative people

Happy is the servant who does not talk in order to receive a reward. He does not reveal everything he is and he is not prone to being talkative. He wisely weighs his words and his replies to other people. Woe to the religious person who does not keep in the depth of his heart the favours which the Lord has lavished on him. Woe to the person who does not show these favours to the world through his holy life. Woe to him if he seeks to profit from these favours and makes them known to others only through his words. This is the only reward he will receive and his hearers will derive little benefit from his words.

## 23 True correction

Happy is the servant who receives warnings, accusations and reproaches with as much patience as if it came from himself. Happy is the servant who when reproved submits with gentleness, obeys reverently, confesses his fault humbly and makes amends willingly. Happy is the servant who is not eager to excuse himself and who humbly bears shame and reproach for a fault he has not committed.

## 24 True humility

Happy is the person who is found to be as humble among his subjects as among his superiors.

Happy is the servant who always lives under the rod of correction. 'The faithful and wise servant' (Matt. 24:45) promptly expiates all his sins, by inner contrition, outward confession and deeds of reparation.

## 25 True love

Happy is the religious person who loves the brother who is sick and unable to be useful to him as much as he loves the person who is well and capable of doing him service. Happy is the brother who loves and respects his own absent brother as if he were present with him. Happy is the brother who never says anything behind his brother's back that he would not in love say to his face.

## 26 God's servants should honour clerics

Happy is the servant who places his confidence in clerics who live according to the way of the holy Roman Church. Woe to those who despise clerics. Clerics may be sinners but no one should despise them because the right to judge them is reserved for the Lord. The most holy body and blood of our Lord Jesus Christ is placed in their care. Clerics alone receive and give to others. As clerics are in a more responsible position than other people any sin committed against them is greater than sins committed against other people.

## 27 Virtues replacing vices

Where charity and wisdom reign there is neither fear nor ignorance. Where patience and humility reign there is neither anger nor disturbance. Where poverty and joy are found there is neither love of money nor avarice. There is neither anxiety nor prodigality where peace and meditation reign. Where the fear of God guards the heart the enemy can find no door to enter. Where mercy and temperance live there is neither superfluity nor harshness.

## 28 Hiding good for fear of losing it

The servant who stores up God's blessings for himself in heaven is happy. He does not try to make capital out of them as he passes on these blessings to the world. The most high God himself will reveal these deeds to those people he chooses to. Blessed is the servant who keeps the secrets of the Lord in his heart.

[St Francis often said, 'When God's servant receives a visit from on high while he is praying, he should say: "O Lord, thou hast sent me this consolation from heaven, even though I am an unworthy sinner. I return it to your safe keeping, otherwise I would think that I am robbing treasure from you." When God's servant continues to pray he must think of himself as a poor little thing and a sinner, just as if he had not received any blessing.']

# Part II

# LETTERS

# LETTER TO ALL THE FAITHFUL

Your servant and subject Brother Francis pays his respects to all Christians, clerics, lay brothers, men and women and to all who live in the world. May you know the true peace of heaven and sincere charity in the Lord.

Being the servant of all, I am obliged to serve every one and communicate to all the balm-bearing words of my Lord. I am writing this letter to you because of the weakness of my body which makes it impossible for me to visit you. This letter will be my messenger to tell you again the sayings of our Lord Jesus Christ, the Word of the Father and the words of the Holy Spirit which are 'spirit and life' (John 6:64).

## 1 The Word of the Father

God most high announced the coming of this holy, great and glorious Word of the Father. He did this through the archangel St Gabriel to the blessed and glorious virgin Mary, in whose womb Christ received the real body of our humanity and frailty. Although he was richer than anybody else he was willing with his ever-blessed mother to choose poverty.

When his passion was near he celebrated the Passover with his disciples. 'And taking bread, he gave thanks, blessed and brake it, saying: Take ye, and eat: This is my

77

body. And taking the chalice, he said: This is my blood of
the New Testament, which shall be shed for you and for
many unto remission of sins' (see Matt. 26:26–28; Luke
22:19–20).

Invoking the Father, he uttered this prayer, 'My Father,
if it be possible, let this chalice pass from me' (Matt.
26:39). 'And his sweat became as drops of blood, trickling
down upon the ground' (Luke 22:44). However, he gave
up his will to the will of the Father, saying, 'Father, . . .
thy will be done'; 'not as I will, but as thou wilt' (Matt.
26:42, 39).

Now the Father's will was that his blessed and glorious
Son, whom he gave to be born for us, should offer himself
with his own blood as a sacrifice and victim on the altar of
the cross. This sacrifice was not for his own sins, for everything was made through him. This sacrifice was for our
sins, and he has left us an example that we should walk in
his steps (John 1:3; 1 Pet. 2:21). Christ desires that we
should all be saved by him and that we should receive him
with a pure heart and a chaste body. Alas, there are very
few who receive him and wish to be saved by him, even
though 'his yoke is sweet and his burden light' (see Matt.
11:30).

## 2 People who break God's commandments

People who refuse to taste how sweet the Lord is, and
prefer darkness to light and who do not wish to follow
God's commands are cursed. The psalmist writes about
such people, 'They are cursed who decline from thy commandments' (Ps. 119:21). On the other hand, how happy
and blessed are those who love the Lord and serve him.
As the Lord himself points out in the Gospel, 'Thou shalt
love the Lord thy God with thy whole heart, and with thy
whole soul, and . . . thy neighbour as thyself' (Matt.
22:37–39).

## 3 The love of God and worshipping God

Yes, let us love God, let us worship him with a pure heart and a pure mind, for that is what he seeks above everything else. He says, 'The true adorers shall adore the Father in spirit and in truth. . . . They that adore him, must adore him in spirit and in truth' (John 4:23–24). Let us offer him our prayers and praise day and night, saying, 'Our Father, who art in heaven' (Matt. 6:9), for 'we ought always to pray, and not to faint' (Luke 18:1).

## 4 Confessing our sins to a priest

We must also confess all our sins to the priest and receive at his hands the body and blood of our Lord Jesus Christ. The person who does not eat his body and drink his blood cannot enter the kingdom of God. But let us eat and drink it worthily, for, 'he that eateth and drinketh unworthily eateth and drinketh judgement to himself, not discerning the body of the Lord' (1 Cor. 11:29), that is to say, he does not distinguish it from other food.

Moreover, let us bring forth 'fruits worthy of penance' (Luke 3:8). Let us love our neighbour as ourselves, and if anyone cannot or will not do so, at least let him do him no evil but seek to do him good.

## 5 How those who judge should judge

Let those who are invested with the authority of justice exercise it with mercy and in the same compassionate way as they themselves would wish to be treated by the Lord. For let 'judgement without mercy' be shown 'to him that hath not done mercy' (Jas. 2:13). Let us be charitable and humble, let us give alms and wash our soul from the stains of sin. People lose everything they leave in this world except for the fruits of their charity and the alms they have scattered. The Lord will give them recompense and a just reward.

## 6 Spiritual and bodily fasting

We must also fast, avoid vices and sins, and superfluity in eating and drinking. We must remain attached to the catholic church. We must frequently visit churches. We must reverence the clerics, not for themselves if they are sinners, but because of their office and ministry of the most holy body and blood of our Lord Jesus Christ, whom they sacrifice on the altar and receive and distribute to others. Let us be fully convinced that no one can be saved except by this blood of our Lord Jesus Christ and by the words of the Lord. The clerics proclaim, announce and spread these words of Christ and only they minister in this way. Members of religious communities, who have renounced the world, are bound to do more and greater things, but 'not to leave the other undone' (Luke 11:42).

## 7 How we must love our enemies and do them good

We must hate our body, its vices and sins, for the Lord says in the Gospel, 'an evil man out of the evil treasure [of his heart] bringeth forth that which is evil' (Luke 6:45). We must love our enemies and do good to those who hate us (see Luke 6:27). We must follow the precepts and counsels of our Lord Jesus Christ. We must deny ourselves, placing our body under the yoke of holy obedience and servitude, according to our vows promised to the Lord.

## 8 Let him who is in authority be humble

No one is duty bound to obey any order which is wrong or

sinful. Let him who is the greatest and has the right to command consider himself as the lowest and the servant of the other brothers. Let him show to each person the same mercy which he would wish to receive himself in similar circumstances. Let him not become angry with a brother because of his offence. With all patience and humility he must encourage the brother and warn him with kindness.

## 9 Fleeing from the wisdom of the world

We must not be wise and prudent by the standards of the world, but simple, humble and pure. Let us keep our body under subjection and in contempt because we are all through our own fault corrupt and miserable and vile worms of the earth. As the Lord says through the psalmist, 'I am a worm, and no man: the reproach of men, and the outcast of the people' (Ps. 22:6). We must never seek to dominate others but be servants and subject to other people, 'to every human creature for God's sake' (1 Pet. 2:13). May the spirit of the Lord rest on everyone who behaves and perseveres to the end in this way. May God dwell in the lives of such people. They will be the sons of the heavenly Father as they carry out his wishes. They are the husbands, wives, brothers and mothers of our Lord Jesus Christ. We are married to Christ when our soul is sanctified and united to Jesus Christ through the Holy Spirit. We are his brothers when we do the will of his heavenly Father. We are his mothers when we cherish him in our heart and in our body through pure love and a clean conscience. We do this as we do holy actions for Christ's sake which are an example to others.

Oh, what glory, what dignity and what splendour it is to have a Father in heaven! How glorious, how beautiful and how sweet it is to have a Spouse in heaven! What splendour, what charm, what happiness, what peace, what sweetness, what inner joy and what supreme fortune it is to have such a Brother! He gives his life for his sheep. He has prayed to the Father for us, saying, 'Holy Father, keep them in thy name whom thou hast given me. Father, all those whom thou hast given me in the world were thine, and thou hast given them to me, and the words which thou gavest me, I have given to them, and they have received them, and have known in very deed that I came out from thee; and they have believed that thou didst send me. I pray for them: I pray not for the world; bless them, sanctify them. And for them do I sanctify myself: that they also may be sanctified in one, as we also are. . . . Father, I will that where I am, they also whom thou hast given me may be with me, and may see my glory in thy kingdom' (see John 17:6–24).

## 10 The praise due to God

Let every creature in heaven and earth, in the sea and in the depths, give honour, praise, blessing and glory to God. For Christ has suffered so much for us, and has given us so many blessings and will procure so many more for us in the future. He alone is our might and he alone is good. He alone is most high, all-powerful and worthy to be praised. He alone is holy and glorious. He alone is blessed and praised from everlasting to everlasting, world without end. Amen.

## 11 Penance

But alas, the following people do not see the true light of our Lord Jesus Christ: all those who do not live in penitence and who do not receive the body and blood of our Lord Jesus Christ; all those who live in vice and sin, following the lead of their evil passions and their base desires; all those who obey the world, the desires of the body and the claims and demands of this world; all those who are deceived by the devil and give way to him in their hearts and do his deeds as his sons.

They ignore spiritual wisdom and do not have with them the Son of God who is the true wisdom of the Father. They see, they know and yet they do evil. They deliberately lose their souls. Listen to this, you who are blind and have been dazzled by your enemies, the world, the flesh and the devil. Sin flatters the body and it hates serving God. All vices and sins, according to the Gospel, come from the heart (Matt. 15:19).

You will never have any lasting treasure either in this world or in the next world. You imagine that you will enjoy the vanities of this world for a long time but you are deceiving yourself. For the day and the hour is approaching which you will not contemplate and which you ignore.

## 12 Dying impenitent

The body is sick and death approaches. The assembled relatives and friends say, 'Make your will.' His wife, children, relations, and friends pretend to weep. The sick man sees them weeping and is moved by a bad emotion. He thinks to himself: 'Yes, my soul, my body, all my goods, I leave them in your hands.' Whoever bequeaths his soul, body and all his goods into such hands is truly cursed. Also the Lord says through his prophet, 'Cursed be the man that trusteth in man' (Jer. 17:5).

Then they send for a priest and the priest says, 'Will you do penance for your sins?'

The sick man replies, 'I will.'

'Will you make amends for your errors, frauds and injustices from your own money, in as far as you are able?'

'No,' the sick man responds.

'Why not?' the priest asks.

'Because I have given all my money and goods into the

hands of my friends and relatives,' says the dying man.

Quite soon after this the man is no longer able to talk and so the miserable person dies his bitter death.

Let everyone fully understand what happens to a man, whoever he may be, who dies in his sins and crimes and who has not made expiation for them. If this person has had the opportunity to repent and refuses to do so then the devil tears his soul from his body. Only those who have experienced this know the degree of pain that is inflicted by the devil as he does this. All talents, power, wisdom and knowledge he thought he possessed are taken from him. His relatives and friends seize his fortune, share it out, and later say, 'Cursed be the soul of him who might have enriched himself more than he has done, and have left us more.' Meanwhile, the worms are gnawing his body. This is how he loses his soul and body in this short life. He is now in hell where he will undergo eternal judgement.

In the name of the Father, and of the Son, and of the Holy Spirit. Amen. To all those who shall see this letter, I, Brother Francis, your little servant, beg and implore you by God's love, and with the desire to kiss your feet, to receive lovingly these fragrant words of our Lord Jesus Christ. I humbly call on you to put these words into practice and to obey them totally. Those who are not able to read must have these words read to them frequently. They must keep them in their hearts wherever they go. They must diligently endeavour to follow them to their life's end as they are spirit and life. People who do not do this will give an account on the day of judgement to the tribunal of Christ. Everybody who accepts them and understands them must communicate them to others. They must persevere to the end in putting them into practice. Blessed be the Father, the Son and the Holy Spirit. Amen.

# LETTER TO THE CHAPTER-GENERAL AND ALL THE FRIARS

In the name of the sovereign trinity and of the holy unity, Father, Son and Holy Spirit. Amen.

Brother Francis, a wretched and fallen man, your little servant, sends his greetings in Christ who has redeemed and washed us in his precious blood. Brother Francis greets all his revered and well-loved friars, his master the minister-general of the Order of the Minors, and the ministers who shall succeed him, and all his humble, simple and obedient brothers in Christ who have been and who are yet to come. At the mention of Christ's name, adore him with fear and reverence and prostrate yourselves on the ground. The Lord Jesus Christ, the Son of the most high God, this is the name which is blessed throughout all ages. Amen.

Listen, my lords, my sons and my brothers, give ear to my words. Incline the voice of your heart and obey the voice of the Son of God. Keep his commandments with all your heart and follow his counsels with your whole mind. Praise him, for he is good, and extol him through your deeds. He has sent you into the whole world to bear witness to his word, through your own word and through your deeds, and to make known to everyone that there is nobody else who is almighty like Christ. Persevere in a life of virtue and holy obedience. Keep your vows faithfully and with a generous heart. As for the children, the Lord God offers himself to you.

## 1 Reverence due to the holy sacrament

I implore you, my brothers, as I kiss your feet, and with
the complete affection in my heart I beseech you to show
the greatest possible reverence and honour to the most
holy body and blood of our Lord Jesus Christ. For it is
through Christ that all things on earth and in heaven have
been restored to peace and have been reconciled to the
almighty Father (see Col. 1:20).

## 2 The mass

In the Lord, I also implore all my friars who are, shall be,
or who desire to be priests of the most high God, that,
when they desire to celebrate mass, they are pure. For
they offer the true sacrifice of the most holy body and
blood of our Lord Jesus Christ. They must do so reverently and worthily, with a holy and pure intention. They
must have no earthly motives such as fear or the desire to
please people as if they could please anybody. Let their
whole intention, as much as the grace of the Almighty
allows, be directed to the sovereign Lord alone. Let them
seek to please him only, for he alone works there in a
pleasing way, for he says, 'Do this for a commemoration
of me' (Luke 22:19). When anyone acts in a different way
he becomes another traitor, Judas. Then 'he is guilty of
the body and blood of the Lord' (1 Cor. 11:27).

Remember, priests, my brothers, what is written in the
law of Moses. Those who broke this law, even in an outward way, were condemned to death without mercy by the
decree of the Lord (see Heb. 10:28). 'How much more, do
you think he deserveth worse punishments, who hath
trodden under foot the Son of God, and hath esteemed
the blood of the testament unclean, by which he was
sanctified, and hath offered an affront to the Spirit of
grace!' (Heb. 10:29). Man, indeed, despises, defiles and

tramples under foot the Lamb of God when, as the apostle Paul says (see 1 Cor. 11:29), he does not distinguish or discern the holy bread of Christ from other food when he eats unworthily. So even though he may be in a state of grace he fails to communicate profitably. Thus the Lord says through his prophet, 'Cursed be he that doth the work of the Lord deceitfully' (Jer. 48:10). He despises the priests who will not wholeheartedly strive to avoid these faults and even says that he will curse their blessings.

Listen, my brothers. The most blessed virgin Mary is correctly honoured because she bore the Lord as a virgin in her womb. John the Baptist trembled at the thought of laying his hand on the head of the Man-God. The tomb where Christ rested for a few hours is venerated. So how much more then should he be considered holy, just and worthy who touches Christ with his hands and takes Christ into his mouth and heart? For he who now gives Christ to others is no longer giving a mortal Christ but a gloriously victorious Christ who is now worshipped for evermore by the angels.

Consider your calling, you brothers who are priests, and be holy because God is holy (see Lev. 11:44). Just as the Lord God has honoured you above everyone else for this ministry so you should love, adore and honour him the more. It is a terrible mistake and a miserable fault to have Christ so close to you and for you to be thinking of anything else in the world. May the whole world be gripped in fear, may all people tremble, may the heavens exult when, in the hands of the priests, the Christ the Son of the living God descends upon the altar. Oh amazing splendour, astounding condescension! Oh sublime humility! The Master of the universe, God himself and the Son of God, humbles himself so much that he hides himself for our salvation under the feeble appearance of bread. See, brothers, the humility of God and pour out your hearts before him. Humble yourselves so that, in due course, you may be exalted by Christ. Keep nothing of yourselves to yourselves. Then Christ may completely possess you as he has wholly given himself to you.

## 3 Celebrate only one mass a day

I therefore warn my friars, I beseech them in the Lord, that wherever they are they should only celebrate one mass a day. This should be celebrated according to the rite of the holy church. If, however, there are many priests, let one be content through love and charity to hear mass from another, because the Lord Jesus Christ makes up to all who are worthy, whether they are present or absent. Christ is found in many places and yet is not divided as he does not suffer any diminution. Everywhere he is the same united person working as he wills with the Lord God the Father and the Holy Spirit the Comforter, throughout all ages. Amen.

## 4 Respect for the holy scriptures

'He that is of God heareth the words of God' (John 8:47). We who are specially entrusted with divine offices not only hear but perform the word of God. So because we are additionally imbued with the grandeur of our Creator and with our subjection to him we take great care of the sacred vessels and other things which we use to contain his word. Therefore, I warn all my friars and strengthen them in Christ. Wherever they may find these written words they are to venerate them as well as they are able. If these words are not carefully kept, or if they lie scattered around in some unsuitable place, the friars are to collect them together. They are to place them in a worthy place, honouring in them the Lord who spoke them. Many things are made holy by the word of God and through the words of Christ the altar's sacrament is effected.

# 5 Confession

I confess all my sins to God the Father, Son and Holy Spirit. I confess all my sins to the ever-blessed virgin Mary and to all the saints in heaven and on earth. I confess all my sins to the minister-general of our Order as he is my revered lord. I confess all my sins to all the priests of our Order and to all my other blessed brothers. In many ways I have sinned through my own fault. I have not observed the Rule which I promised to the Lord. I have not said the Office according to the instructions in the Rule because of neglect, sickness or ignorance.

# 6 The Rule, the Office and singing

I earnestly beseech my master, Brother Elias, minister-general, to see that everyone always observes the Rule. The clerics are to say the Office devoutly before God. They must pay attention to the thoughts of their heart rather than to the sound of their voice. The voice must be united with the thoughts and these thoughts must be united to God. Then, by the purity of their conscience, they will please God rather than soothe other people's ears through the voluptuousness of their voice. As for me, I promise, as the Lord shall give me grace, to observe these points carefully. I shall leave it to the brothers who are with me to observe all these rules as they say the Office and as they engage in other regular spiritual exercises. If any friars refuse to observe these instructions I shall no longer regard them as Catholics nor as brothers. I do not want to see them or speak to them until they have done penance. This applies to everybody else who neglects the Rule and abandons discipline. Our Lord Jesus Christ gave his life in case he might not be obedient enough to his most holy Father.

I, Brother Francis, an unprofitable and unworthy creature

of the Lord God, in the Lord Jesus Christ beseech Brother Elias, minister of our whole religion, to keep this writing in your possession. You are to respect it and to put it into practice. This also applies to all ministers-general who succeed Brother Elias and all other custodians and guardians of friars, both present and future. I beg you all to guard jealously what is contained in it, to ensure that it is diligently observed as long as the world lasts, according to the good pleasure of almighty God.

Blessed are ye in the Lord, ye who do this, and may the Lord be with you through all eternity. Amen.

# LETTER TO A MINISTER

[Celano said the following about St Francis: 'His whole philosophy, his whole desire as long as he lived, his sole wish was constantly to seek, among wise and simple, perfect and imperfect, the means to walk in the way of truth and to become more perfect.']

To Brother N., minister, may the Lord bless you.

I admonish you as best I can on the subject of your salvation. You should think positively about the things which hinder your love of the Lord God: the people who annoy you, brothers and other people, even if they went as far as hitting you. Desire God's salvation and nothing else. You will achieve this through the spirit of true obedience to the Lord God and to me for I am certain that in this lies true obedience. You are to love the people who behave to you in this way. You should only desire from them what the Lord teaches you to look for. Concentrate your love in wishing them to be better Christians. Seek that rather than a hermitage. I desire that you love the Lord and me, God's servant and yours, as you observe this advice. When a brother seeks you out make sure that he leaves you with a message of compassion, no matter how guilty he is. If he does not seek pardon suggest to him that he should be seeking pardon. Even if he should come to you after this more than one thousand times you should love him more than you love me. You are to draw him to the

Lord and always have compassion on him. When you have the opportunity tell the guardians that you have decided to behave in this way.

Concerning mortal sins: If any brother, at the instigation of the enemy, sins mortally, he must go to his guardian. All the brothers who know about his fault must guard against speaking badly of him or making him feel ashamed. They should show the brother kindness and not expose his sin. 'They that are in health need not a physician, but they that are ill' (Matt. 9:12). They should send him to his guardian with a companion. The guardian should welcome him with kindness and treat him in the way he would wish to be treated if he himself were in a similar situation.

If a brother commits a venial sin he should confess it to a brother priest. If no priest is available he should confess to any other brother. When a priest is found he should confess to him and be absolved. Confessors have no right whatsoever to impose any other penance that this, 'Go, and sin no more' (John 8:11).

Keep this letter with you until Pentecost so that it may be followed. You must attend the chapter with your brothers. With the help of the Lord you must endeavour to receive enlightenment on these points and on those which are less explicit in the Rule.

# LETTER TO THE RULERS OF THE PEOPLE

Brother Francis, your wretched little servant in the Lord, wishes all the chiefs, consuls, judges and governors of all countries and everyone else who receives this letter, salvation and peace.

Consider and observe that the day of death is approaching (see Gen. 47:29). I urge you then, with all possible respect, not to forget the Lord or to deviate from his commandments as you live surrounded by the cares and anxieties of this world. Everybody who forgets God and strays from his commandments is cursed. God will forget such people. When the day of death does come everything that these people think they possess will be taken from them. The more powerful and the more they were held in high esteem in this world the more bitter will be their torments in hell.

I also urgently counsel you, my lords, to set aside all care and anxiety. You must lovingly receive the most holy body and blood of our Lord Jesus Christ in holy remembrance of him. The people who are entrusted to your care must pay endless homage to the Lord. Every evening a crier must announce to the people that it is time to give thanks and praise God almighty. Remember that you will have to give account of your actions on the day of judgement to your Lord Jesus Christ if you do not follow these instructions. Everyone who carries out the contents of this letter will be blessed by the Lord God.

# LETTER TO CLERICS

This letter is to clerics about how they are to reverence the Lord's body and keep the altar clean.

All clerics are to note carefully the great sin and ignorance of some people who fail to respect the most holy body and blood of our Lord Jesus Christ. Christ is the most sacred of all people and the written words of consecration must be adhered to. We know that the body of Christ does not exist until after the words of consecration. We possess nothing and we see nothing of the most high God in this world outside the body and blood of Christ. Through Christ's name and word which created us we were brought back from death to life.

Some clerics dabble in these holy mysteries in a light-hearted way. They must carefully examine their dirty chalices, corporals and the linen used in the consecration of the body and blood of our Lord Jesus Christ. Many leave the chalice in unsuitable places and carry it around irreverently and both receive and administer it carelessly. Our Lord Jesus Christ's written words and his titles are sometimes trampled on, for 'The sensual man perceiveth not these things that are of the Spirit of God' (1 Cor. 2:14).

The good Lord places himself in our hands as we handle him and daily receive him. This should move us to be deeply pious. For we need to place ourselves in his hands.

So we must quickly and resolutely correct these faults

- along with our other faults. Whenever the most holy body of our Lord Jesus Christ has been neglected it must be brought back to a sacred place. In the same way if the names of God and his written words are found in an unsuitable place they should be collected and placed in an honourable position. We know that we are bound to observe all these rules. They are the Lord's precepts and regulations of our holy mother the church. Anybody who does not behave in this way must remember that he has to give an account of himself on the day of judgement before our Lord Jesus Christ. Anybody who promotes these writings so that they are better observed will receive the Lord's blessing.

# LETTER TO ALL THE GUARDIANS (1)

Brother Francis, your little servant in the Lord God, greets all the guardians of the Friars Minor who receive this letter. I greet you in the name of these new [eucharistic] signs in heaven and earth which are excellent in God's sight and which many religious people and other people do not understand.

I implore you to ensure that clerics humbly carry out their duties. They should, above everything else, venerate the most holy body and blood of our Lord Jesus Christ, his holy name, his written words and the words of consecration. They must treat the chalices, corporals, the ornaments on the altar and everything that is to do with the sacrament as sacred. If the most holy body of the Lord is placed in an obscure place they are to move it reverently to a more prominent place and to administer it with great care. If the names of the Lord and the written words of the Lord are in a dirty area they are to be moved to a clean area.

You must tell the people to repent when you preach. Warn them that they cannot be saved unless they receive the Lord's most holy body and blood. When the sacrament is carried about during the priestly sacrifice at the altar everyone must kneel, offering praise, honour and glory to the true and living Lord God.

Declare and preach about Christ's splendours to everyone. Then everyone throughout the whole world, as soon as the bells ring, will give thanks and adore the almighty God.

All my brothers who are guardians are to take this letter, keep it and give it to other friars. All preachers and guardians of friars are to make a copy of this letter. They must always preach what it contains so that they may receive the Lord's blessing and mine as a result of true and holy obedience. Amen.

# LETTER TO ALL THE GUARDIANS (2)

Brother Francis, the least of the servants of God, greeting and holy peace in the Lord to all the guardians of the Friars Minor who receive this letter.

Many things that men regard as evil are sublime in God's sight. Many things that are precious and noteworthy in God's sight are regarded as contemptible and repulsive in the sight of men. I beg you to give my letter to the clerics, which refers to the most holy body and blood of our Lord, to the bishops and other clerics. They are to learn my recommendations by heart. Make a large number of copies of my letter to the rulers of the people. This is the letter intended for the rulers, consuls and rectors in which they are instructed to ensure that God's praises are celebrated by the people in public places. Make these copies quickly and give them out. Greetings in the Lord.

# LETTER TO BROTHER LEO

Brother Leo, desire salvation and peace for your Brother Francis!

Yes, I speak to you, my son, as mother, and all that we have said as we travelled I will say again briefly in this letter. I am going to give you some advice about what to do if you want my counsel in the future. Work out the best way to please the Lord God. Follow in his steps and in his poverty. Embrace this way of life with the Lord God's blessing and in obedience to me. If you seek consolation or have any other spiritual reason for visiting me, do come, Leo.

# LITTLE LETTER TO BROTHER LEO

## Praises of God

Thou, Lord and God, art holy, who alone workest miracles. Thou art strong. Thou art great. Thou art the most high God. Thou art the all-powerful King, the holy Father, the Lord of heaven and earth. Thou art the Lord God, three in one, the universal good. Thou art goodness, universal and supreme, the true and living Lord God. Thou art benevolence and love. Thou art wisdom. Thou art humility. Thou art patience. Thou art security. Thou art peace. Thou art joy and gladness. Thou art justice and temperance. Thou art all riches which satisfy.

Thou art beauty. Thou art grace. Thou art our Protector. Thou art our Keeper and Defender. Thou art our might. Thou art our refreshment. Thou art our hope. Thou art our confidence. Thou art our immense sweetness. Thou art our eternal life, our great and adorable Lord, almighty God, merciful Saviour.

## A blessing for Brother Leo

May the Lord bless thee and keep thee. May he show his face to thee, and have mercy on thee. May he turn his countenance to thee and give thee peace. God bless thee, Brother Leo T.

[To these words Brother Leo added in red ink: 'The most blessed Francis, two years before he died, spent Lent at Alverna in honour of the most blessed virgin Mary, mother of God, and of the most blessed archangel Michael. He stayed there from the feast of the Assumption of the holy virgin Mary to the feast of St Michael in September. The hand of the Lord was on him throughout this time. He had the vision and conversation with the Seraphim as well as the impression of the wounds of Christ on his body. He wrote these prayers on the back of this little sheet with his own hand as he gave thanks to the Lord for the favour he had been granted.']

# LETTER TO BROTHER ELIAS (1)

To the reverend father in Christ, to Brother Elias, Vicar of the whole Order. Brother Francis sends his greetings in Christ to you.

Brother, may the Lord give you his holy blessing. Always be patient and full of kindness. If your brothers wrong you, offer it to God. I know only one way to bring back an erring brother to God and that is to show him God's kindness. Never stop loving the brother who sins gravely. If he will not approach you on account of his own fear ask him if he wishes to receive pardon. If a brother, urged by the devil, falls into grievous sin, let him seek the guardian, who must send him to the provincial, who will receive him with mercy. If the provincial finds that he is penitent then he must say, 'Go, and sin no more.' Greetings in the Lord.

# LETTER TO BROTHER ELIAS (2)

To the reverend father in Christ, to Brother Elias, Vicar of the whole Order. Brother Francis sends his greetings in Christ to you.

In all your actions, Brother Elias, I recommend, above everything else, charity and patience. You should show yourself to be most tolerant. The burden you bear on your shoulders is great and heavy since it is the eternal salvation of a multitude of people. In the ancient law the high priest had the names of the twelve tribes of Israel on the breastplate of judgement which hung from his shoulders down his chest. This signifies that a prelate bears his subjects on his shoulders. He must also bear them in his heart. He would not be able to be tolerant towards those he had stopped loving. When our Lord Jesus Christ was about to entrust his church to Peter he examined the apostle's charity before handing over his sheep to him.

Keep watch, therefore, in case any brother sins. If one of the brothers commits a fault he should not leave you without amending his life or being pardoned for his sin. As you are a doctor offer a remedy to the sick. As the Lord says, those who are well do not need a healer, but those who are sick. Watch, warn, work, feed, love, wait and fear. Greetings in the Lord.

# LETTER TO JACQUELINE OF SETTESOLI

To the Lady Jacqueline, servant of the most high God, Brother Francis, Christ's little poor one, sends greetings in the Lord and union in the Holy Spirit.

Understand, most dear one, that the blessed Christ, in his goodness, has revealed to me that my life is near its end. So if you wish to see me again alive you must come quickly to St Mary of the Angels as soon as you have received this letter. If you do not come before Saturday you will not find me alive. Bring with you a hair-cloth sheet as a shroud for my body and bring wax for the burial. I beseech you also to bring me some of the food you used to give me when I was ill in Rome. . . .

[This letter is unfinished.]

# LETTER TO ST ANTONY

To my well-beloved Brother Antony. Brother Francis
sends you greetings in the Lord.

It will please me if you instruct the brothers the teach-
ings of holy theology. But do this in such a way that you do
not damage in yourself or others the spirit of holy prayer
which we engage in according to the Rule. Adieu.

[St Francis was asked if he would like learned brothers
who had already been received into the Order to diligently
study the holy scriptures. St Francis replied: 'I approve of
this provided that they follow Christ's example in this. We
are told that Christ preferred prayer to reading. So these
brothers must not neglect the spirit of prayer. They must
not study in order to become learned orators; rather, they
should study so that they can put into practice in their own
lives what they learn. Then, when they have done this
themselves, they can suggest other people do the same. I
want my friars to be true disciples of the gospel and to
advance so much in the knowledge of the truth that they
may grow in purity and innocence. They are not to separate the innocence of the dove from the wisdom of the ser-
pent since these virtues were united in our good Master's
teaching.]

# Part III

# THE OFFICE OF THE LORD'S PASSION

These are the Psalms which our most blessed father Francis selected to honour, commemorate and praise the Lord's passion. They start at Compline on the Thursday of the Lord's Supper, since on that night our Lord Jesus Christ was betrayed and arrested. For this office the most blessed Francis began by reciting the prayer that our Lord and Master taught us, 'Our Father, most holy,' etc., together with the praises, 'Holy, holy, holy.'

When the Lauds and prayer were ended, Francis began with the antiphon, 'Holy virgin Mary,' etc. The Office started and ended with the antiphon.

# 1

# THE OFFICE OF THE LORD'S PASSION FOR THE THREE LAST DAYS OF HOLY WEEK AND THE VIGILS DURING THE YEAR

## At Compline

*Antiphon*

Holy virgin Mary, there is no one in the world like you, no woman who has been born in the world is like you. You are the daughter and handmaid of the most high King, the heavenly Father. You are the mother of our most holy Lord Jesus Christ, spouse of the Holy Spirit. Pray for us, with St Michael the archangel and all the virtues of heaven and all the saints around your dear and most holy Son, our Lord and Master.

*Psalm*

O God, I have declared my life to thee: thou hast set my tears in thy sight.

All my enemies seek to do me evil: they have met together in council to do so.

They have rendered evil for good and hatred for my affection.

Instead of loving me they scorned me, I myself prayed for them.

O my holy Father, King of heaven and earth, do not forsake me: tribulation is nigh, and there is no one to help.

My enemies turn their backs upon me whenever I cry to thee: but I know that thou art my God.

My friends and my relations drew nigh and rose up against me: my neighbours stood afar off.

Thou hast put far away from me those that know me; they have looked upon me as an object of horror: I was delivered up and came not forth.

Holy Father, take not from me thy help: O my God, look upon me and help me.

Attend unto my help, Lord, the God of my salvation.

Glory be to the Father, and to the Son, and to the Holy Spirit. As it was in the beginning, is now, and ever shall be, world without end. Amen.

*Antiphon*

Holy virgin Mary, there is no one in the world like you, no woman who has been born in the world is like you. You are the daughter and handmaid of the most high King, the heavenly Father. You are the mother of our most holy Lord Jesus Christ, spouse of the Holy Spirit. Pray for us, with St Michael the archangel and all the virtues of heaven and all the saints around your dear and most holy Son, our Lord and Master.

Glory be to the Father, and to the Son, and to the Holy Spirit. As it was in the beginning, is now, and ever shall be, world without end. Amen.

This antiphon is said at all the Hours. It serves as antiphon, little chapter, hymn, verse and collect at Matins and at all the other Hours. The most blessed Francis said nothing else except this antiphon and the psalms for his Hours.

At the end of the Office he said, 'Let us bless the living and true God. Let us ascribe to him always praise, honour, glory, blessing and everything that is good. Amen.'

## At Matins

*Antiphon*

Holy virgin Mary, there is no one in the world like you, no woman who has been born in the world is like you. You are the daughter and handmaid of the most high King, the heavenly Father. You are the mother of our most holy Lord Jesus Christ, spouse of the Holy Spirit. Pray for us, with St Michael the archangel and all the virtues of heaven and all the saints around your dear and most holy Son, our Lord and Master.

*Psalm (see Ps. 18)*

O Lord God of my salvation, I have cried before thee day and night.

Let my prayer come in before thee: incline thine ear to my petition.

Pity my soul and deliver it: save me because of mine enemies.

For thou, who hast drawn me out of the womb, thou art my hope from the breasts of my mother: from my birth I have been cast into thine arms.

Thou art my God from my mother's womb, be not far from me.

Thou knowest my troubles, the awe and reverence I have for thee.

All my persecutors are before thee: my heart awaits shame and misery.

I looked for one that would grieve together with me: I sought a comforter, and found none.

O God, the wicked have risen up against me, the multitude of the mighty have sought to ruin my soul: they have not set thee before their eyes.

I am counted among them that go down to the pit, I am become as a man without help, free among the dead.

Thou art my most holy Father, my King and my God.

Attend unto me to help me, Lord God of my salvation.

Glory be to the Father, and to the Son, and to the Holy Spirit. As it was in the beginning, is now, and ever shall be, world without end. Amen.

*Antiphon*
Holy virgin Mary, there is no one in the world like you, no woman who has been born in the world is like you. You are the daughter and handmaid of the most high King, the heavenly Father. You are the mother of our most holy Lord Jesus Christ, spouse of the Holy Spirit. Pray for us, with St Michael the archangel and all the virtues of heaven and all the saints around your dear and most holy Son, our Lord and Master.

## At Prime

*Antiphon*
Holy virgin Mary, there is no one in the world like you, no woman who has been born in the world is like you. You are the daughter and handmaid of the most high King, the heavenly Father. You are the mother of our most holy Lord Jesus Christ, spouse of the Holy Spirit. Pray for us, with St Michael the archangel and all the virtues of heaven and all the saints around your dear and most holy Son, our Lord and Master.

*Psalm (see Ps. 57)*
Have mercy on me, O God, have mercy on me: for my soul trusteth in thee.

And in the shadow of thy wings will I hope, until iniquity pass away.

I will cry to God the most high: to God who hath done good to me.

He hath sent from heaven and delivered me, he hath covered my persecutors with shame.

God hath sent his power and his truth, he hath delivered

my soul from the fury of mine enemies and of those who hated me: they made themselves strong against me.

They laid snares for my feet, and have threatened my life.

They dug a pit before my face, and they are fallen into it.

My heart is ready, O God, my heart is ready. I will sing and rehearse a psalm.

Arise, O my glory, arise psaltery and harp: I will arise early.

I will give praise to thee, O Lord, among the people: I will sing a psalm to thee among the nations.

For thy mercy is magnified even to the heavens, and thy truth unto the clouds.

Be thou exalted, O God, above the heavens, and thy glory above all the earth.

Glory be to the Father, and to the Son, and to the Holy Spirit. As it was in the beginning, is now, and ever shall be, world without end. Amen.

*Antiphon*
Holy virgin Mary, there is no one in the world like you, no woman who has been born in the world is like you. You are the daughter and handmaid of the most high King, the heavenly Father. You are the mother of our most holy Lord Jesus Christ, spouse of the Holy Spirit. Pray for us, with St Michael the archangel and all the virtues of heaven and all the saints around your dear and most holy Son, our Lord and Master.


**At Terce**

*Antiphon*
Holy virgin Mary, there is no one in the world like you, no woman who has been born in the world is like you. You are the daughter and handmaid of the most high King, the

heavenly Father. You are the mother of our most holy Lord Jesus Christ, spouse of the Holy Spirit. Pray for us, with St Michael the archangel and all the virtues of heaven and all the saints around your dear and most holy Son, our Lord and Master.

*Psalm*

Have mercy on me, O God, for man hath trodden me underfoot: all day long he has afflicted me, fighting against me.

All day long have mine enemies trodden me underfoot; they fought against me in great numbers.

All mine enemies have sought me to hurt me, they have desired evil against me.

Those who defended me have taken counsel together against me.

They went out and talked together.

At the sight of me all mocked, they moved their lips and shook their heads.

As for me I am a worm and no man, the scorn of men and the outcast of the people.

I am become a reproach among all my enemies and very much of neighbours, and a fear of my acquaintance.

Holy Father, take not thy help from me, watch over me to protect me.

Attend unto my help, O Lord God of my salvation.

Glory be to the Father, and to the Son, and to the Holy Spirit. As it was in the beginning, is now, and ever shall be, world without end. Amen.

*Antiphon*

Holy virgin Mary, there is no one in the world like you, no woman who has been born in the world is like you. You are the daughter and handmaid of the most high King, the heavenly Father. You are the mother of our most holy Lord Jesus Christ, spouse of the Holy Spirit. Pray for us, with St Michael the archangel and all the virtues of heaven

and all the saints around your dear and most holy Son, our
Lord and Master.


## At Sext

*Antiphon*
Holy virgin Mary, there is no one in the world like you, no
woman who has been born in the world is like you. You
are the daughter and handmaid of the most high King, the
heavenly Father. You are the mother of our most holy
Lord Jesus Christ, spouse of the Holy Spirit. Pray for us,
with St Michael the archangel and all the virtues of heaven
and all the saints around your dear and most holy Son, our
Lord and Master.


*Psalm (see Pss. 142; 69; 35; 38)*
I have raised my voice to the Lord, I have presented my
prayer to the Lord.

I have offered my supplications before him, and told
him my troubles.

My courage fails me, thou knowest the paths I have followed.

In the way in which I walked they laid a snare for me.

I looked to the right hand and searched, but no one
knew me.

Flight hath failed me, and there is no one that hath
regard to my soul.

For thy sake I have borne reproach; shame has covered
my face.

I am become a stranger to my brethren, and an alien to
the sons of my mother.

Holy Father, the zeal of thy house hath eaten me up:
and the reproaches of them that reproached thee are fallen upon me.

They rejoiced and assembled themselves together
against me; scourges were gathered together upon me,

and I knew not.

They are become more numerous than the hairs of my head; they hated me without a cause.

My enemies and unjust persecutors have grown strong: then did I pay that which I took not away.

False witnesses have risen up, they asked me things that I knew not.

They returned me evil for good, they spake evil of me because I followed goodness.

Thou art my Father most holy, my King and my God.

Attend unto my help, Lord God of my salvation.

Glory be to the Father, and to the Son, and to the Holy Spirit. As it was in the beginning, is now, and ever shall be, world without end. Amen.

*Antiphon*

Holy virgin Mary, there is no one in the world like you, no woman who has been born in the world is like you. You are the daughter and handmaid of the most high King, the heavenly Father. You are the mother of our most holy Lord Jesus Christ, spouse of the Holy Spirit. Pray for us, with St Michael the archangel and all the virtues of heaven and all the saints around your dear and most holy Son, our Lord and Master.

**At None**

*Antiphon*

Holy virgin Mary, there is no one in the world like you, no woman who has been born in the world is like you. You are the daughter and handmaid of the most high King, the heavenly Father. You are the mother of our most holy Lord Jesus Christ, spouse of the Holy Spirit. Pray for us, with St Michael the archangel and all the virtues of heaven and all the saints around your dear and most holy Son, our Lord and Master.

*Psalm*

O all ye that pass by the way, attend and see if there be any sorrow like to my sorrow.

For many dogs have encompassed me, a crowd of wicked ones have fallen upon me.

They looked and stared upon me; they parted my garments among them, and drew lots for my vesture.

They pierced my hands and my feet, they counted all my bones.

They opened their mouth at me like a ravening and roaring lion.

I am poured out like water, and all my bones are scattered.

My heart is become like wax melting in the midst of my bowels.

My strength is dried up like a potsherd, and my tongue hath cleaved to my jaws.

They gave me gall for my food, and in my thirst they gave me vinegar to drink.

They brought me to the dust of death, and they have added to the grief of my wounds.

But I slept and rose up again, and my most holy Father received me with glory.

Holy Father, thou hast taken my right hand, thou hast directed me according to thy will, and thou hast raised me to thy glory.

For what have I in heaven? And besides thee what do I desire upon earth?

See, see that I am God, saith the Lord: I shall be exalted in the midst of the nations, I shall be exalted on the earth.

Blessed be the Lord God of Israel, who hath redeemed the souls of his servants with his own most holy blood. None of those who hope in him shall perish.

And we know that he cometh: he will come to judge justice.

## At Vespers

*Psalm (see Pss. 47; 96)*

O all ye nations, clap your hands, praise God with cries of gladness.

He is the Lord most high and terrible, the King of all the earth.

The most holy, heavenly Father, our King, who before all ages hath sent from on high his dear Son, hath wrought our salvation in the midst of the earth.

Let the heavens rejoice, let the earth be glad, let the sea leap with all that is in it: let the fields be joyful with all they bring forth.

Sing unto him a new song, let the earth praise the Lord.

For the Lord is great and worthy of praise: he is more to be feared than all gods.

Bring to the Lord, O ye kindreds of the Gentiles, bring to the Lord glory and honour, bring to the Lord the glory due to his name.

Bring your own bodies and bear his holy cross, and follow to the end his most holy precepts.

Let all the earth be moved at his presence, proclaim to all nations that the Lord hath reigned.

(The preceding verses are said every day from Good Friday to the Ascension. At the Ascension these are added.)

He has gone up to heaven and sits at the right hand of his most holy Father in heaven.

Be thou exalted, O God, above the heavens, may thy glory be on all the earth.

And we know that he cometh: that he cometh to judge with justice.

(From Ascension to Advent this psalm, 'O all ye nations,' is said in this way with the verses following, the 'Glory be to the Father' is added at the end of the psalm after 'he cometh to judge with justice.'

These psalms are said from Good Friday to Resurrection Sunday as well as from the octave of Pentecost to Advent and from the octave of Epiphany to Holy Thursday, except on Sundays and the greater festivals when they are not said; otherwise they are said every day.)

# 2

# THE OFFICE OF THE LORD'S PASSION
# FOR THE PASCHAL SEASON

## At Compline on Holy Saturday

*Antiphon*
Holy virgin Mary, there is no one in the world like you, no
woman who has been born in the world is like you. You
are the daughter and handmaid of the most high King, the
heavenly Father. You are the mother of our most holy
Lord Jesus Christ, spouse of the Holy Spirit. Pray for us,
with St Michael the archangel and all the virtues of heaven
and all the saints around your dear and most holy Son, our
Lord and Master.

*Psalm (see Ps. 70)*
O God, come to my assistance; Lord, make haste to help
me.

Let them be confounded and ashamed that seek my soul.

Let them be turned backward, and blush for shame that
desire evils to me.

Let them be presently turned away blushing for shame
that say to me: 'Tis well, 'tis well.

Let all that seek thee rejoice and be glad in thee; and let
such as love thy salvation say always: the Lord be magnified.

But I am needy and poor; O God, help me.

Thou art my helper and my deliverer: O Lord, make no delay.

(This psalm is said every day at Compline till the octave of Pentecost.)

## At Matins on Easter Sunday

*Antiphon*
Holy virgin Mary, there is no one in the world like you, no woman who has been born in the world is like you. You are the daughter and handmaid of the most high King, the heavenly Father. You are the mother of our most holy Lord Jesus Christ, spouse of the Holy Spirit. Pray for us, with St Michael the archangel and all the virtues of heaven and all the saints around your dear and most holy Son, our Lord and Master.

*Psalm*
Sing ye to the Lord a new canticle, for he hath done wonderful things.

His right hand hath sanctified his Son, and his arm is holy.

The Lord hath made known his salvation: he hath revealed his justice in the sight of the Gentiles.

On this day the Lord hath commanded his mercy, and a canticle to him in the night.

This is the day that the Lord hath made: let us exult and rejoice in it.

Blessed is he who cometh in the name of the Lord: it is our Lord God, he hath shone upon us.

Let the heavens rejoice, let the earth be glad, let the sea be moved and the fullness thereof, let the fields be joyful with all that are in them.

Bring to the Lord, O ye kindreds of the Gentiles, bring to the Lord glory and honour, bring to the Lord the glory due to his name.

(The above is said from Easter Sunday to the feast of the Ascension every day at all the Hours, except at Vespers, Compline and Prime. On the night of the Ascension these verses (see Ps. 68:33–36) are added.)

Sing to God, ye kingdoms of the earth: sing ye to the Lord, sing ye to God, who mounteth above the heaven of heavens, to the east.

Behold he will give to his voice the voice of power. Give ye glory to God for Israel, his magnificence, and his power is in the clouds.

God is wonderful in his saints. The God of Israel is he who will give power and strength to his people. Blessed be God.

(And note that this psalm from the Ascension of the Lord to the octave of Pentecost is said every day with these verses, at Matins, Terce, Sext and None. The 'Glory be to the Father' is said after 'Blessed be God' and not elsewhere. It is said in the same way only at Matins on Sundays and the main feasts, from the octave of Pentecost to the Thursday of the Lord's Supper as this was the day the Lord ate the Passover with his disciples. Another Psalm may be said at Matins or at Vespers, if desired: 'I will extol thee, O Lord,' as in the Psalter (see Ps. 30). But this is only to be said on the Resurrection Sunday and at the feast of the Ascension.)

## At Prime

*Antiphon*

Holy virgin Mary, there is no one in the world like you, no woman who has been born in the world is like you. You are the daughter and handmaid of the most high King, the heavenly Father. You are the mother of our most holy Lord Jesus Christ, spouse of the Holy Spirit. Pray for us, with St Michael the archangel and all the virtues of heaven and all the saints around your dear and most holy Son, our Lord and Master.

*Psalm (see Ps. 57)*
Have mercy on me, O God, have mercy on me: for my soul trusteth in thee.

And in the shadow of thy wings will I hope, until iniquity pass away.

I will cry to God the most high: to God who hath done good to me.

He hath sent from heaven and delivered me, he hath covered my persecutors with shame.

God hath sent his power and his truth, he hath delivered my soul from the fury of mine enemies and of those who hated me: they made themselves strong against me.

They laid snares for my feet, and have threatened my life.

They dug a pit before my face, and they are fallen into it.

My heart is ready, O God, my heart is ready. I will sing and rehearse a psalm.

Arise, O my glory, arise psaltery and harp: I will arise early.

I will give praise to thee, O Lord, among the people: I will sing a psalm to thee among the nations.

For thy mercy is magnified even to the heavens, and thy truth unto the clouds.

Be thou exalted, O God, above the heavens, and thy glory above all the earth.

Let all the earth be moved at his presence, proclaim to all nations that the Lord hath reigned.

**3**

# THE OFFICE OF THE LORD'S PASSION
# FOR SUNDAYS AND FESTIVALS
# THROUGHOUT THE YEAR

Here begin the other psalms arranged also by our most
blessed father St Francis. They are to be recited instead of
the preceding on Sundays and great festivals from the octave
of the Epiphany to the Thursday of the Lord's Supper.

## At Compline

*Antiphon*
Holy virgin Mary, there is no one in the world like you, no
woman who has been born in the world is like you. You
are the daughter and handmaid of the most high King, the
heavenly Father. You are the mother of our most holy
Lord Jesus Christ, spouse of the Holy Spirit. Pray for us,
with St Michael the archangel and all the virtues of heaven
and all the saints around your dear and most holy Son, our
Lord and Master.

*Psalm (see Ps. 70)*
O God, come to my assistance; Lord, make haste to help
me.

Let them be confounded and ashamed that seek my soul.

Let them be turned backward, and blush for shame that desire evils to me.

Let them be presently turned away blushing for shame that say to me: 'Tis well, 'tis well.

Let all that seek thee rejoice and be glad in thee; and let such as love thy salvation say always: the Lord be magnified.

But I am needy and poor; O God, help me.

Thou art my helper and my deliverer: O Lord, make no delay.

## At Matins

*Antiphon*
Holy virgin Mary, there is no one in the world like you, no woman who has been born in the world is like you. You are the daughter and handmaid of the most high King, the heavenly Father. You are the mother of our most holy Lord Jesus Christ, spouse of the Holy Spirit. Pray for us, with St Michael the archangel and all the virtues of heaven and all the saints around your dear and most holy Son, our Lord and Master.

*Psalm (see Ps. 68:33–36)*
Sing to God, ye kingdoms of the earth: sing ye to the Lord, sing ye to God, who mounteth above the heaven of heavens, to the east.

Behold he will give to his voice the voice of power. Give ye glory to God for Israel, his magnificence, and his power is in the clouds.

God is wonderful in his saints. The God of Israel is he who will give power and strength to his people. Blessed be God.

## At Terce

*Antiphon*

Holy virgin Mary, there is no one in the world like you, no woman who has been born in the world is like you. You are the daughter and handmaid of the most high King, the heavenly Father. You are the mother of our most holy Lord Jesus Christ, spouse of the Holy Spirit. Pray for us, with St Michael the archangel and all the virtues of heaven and all the saints around your dear and most holy Son, our Lord and Master.

*Psalm (see Pss. 17; 65; 72)*

Rejoice all before God, ye inhabitants of the earth, sing a psalm to his name, glorify him and praise him.

Say unto God, how terrible are thy works, O Lord! The greatness of thy power shall confound thine enemies.

Let all the earth adore thee and praise thee, let it sing a psalm to thy name.

Come and listen, all ye who fear the Lord, and I will tell you what great things he hath done for my soul.

I opened my mouth and cried to him, my tongue hath extolled him.

He hath heard my voice from his holy temple, my cry has gone up to him.

Bless our Lord, ye nations, and let your voices be heard to praise him.

All the tribes of the earth shall be blessed in him, all nations shall exalt him.

Blessed be the Lord God of Israel, who only doeth wondrous things.

And blessed be the name of his majesty for ever, and the whole earth shall be filled with his majesty.

**At Sext**

*Antiphon*
Holy virgin Mary, there is no one in the world like you, no woman who has been born in the world is like you. You are the daughter and handmaid of the most high King, the heavenly Father. You are the mother of our most holy Lord Jesus Christ, spouse of the Holy Spirit. Pray for us, with St Michael the archangel and all the virtues of heaven and all the saints around your dear and most holy Son, our Lord and Master.

*Psalm (see Pss. 10; 20; 59)*
May the Lord hear thee in the day of trouble, may the name of the God of Jacob protect thee.

May he send thee help from the sanctuary, and defend thee out of Sion.

May he be mindful of all thy sacrifices, and may thy wholeburned offering be made fat.

May he fulfil the desires of thine heart, and confirm all thy counsels.

We will rejoice in thy salvation, and in the name of our God we shall be exalted.

May the Lord look favourably on all thy petitions; now know I that the Lord hath sent his Son Jesus Christ, and that he will judge the people with justice.

The Lord is become a refuge for the poor, a helper of the needy and persecuted; and let them trust in thee who know thy name.

Blessed be the Lord my God, he is become my help and my refuge in the day of my tribulation.

O my helper, I will sing to thee: God is my help and my defence, my God, my mercy.

## At None

*Antiphon*

Holy virgin Mary, there is no one in the world like you, no woman who has been born in the world is like you. You are the daughter and handmaid of the most high King, the heavenly Father. You are the mother of our most holy Lord Jesus Christ, spouse of the Holy Spirit. Pray for us, with St Michael the archangel and all the virtues of heaven and all the saints around your dear and most holy Son, our Lord and Master.

*Psalm (see Pss. 59; 69; 71)*

In thee, Lord, have I hoped, let me never be put to confusion; deliver me in thy justice, and rescue me.

Incline thine ear unto me, and save me.

Be thou unto me a God, a protector, and a place of strength, that thou mayest make me safe.

For thou art my patience, O Lord, my hope, Lord, from my youth.

Upon thee have I leaned from my mother's womb, thou art my protector ever since I was born: of thee shall I continually sing.

Let my mouth be filled with thy praise; that I may sing thy glory and thy greatness all the day long.

Hear me, O Lord, for thy mercy is kind, look upon me according to the multitude of thy tender mercies.

And turn not away thy face from thy child, for I am in trouble; hear me speedily.

Blessed be the Lord my God; he is become my helper and my refuge in the day of my tribulation.

O my helper, I will sing to thee; God is my defence; my God, my mercy.

## At Vespers

*Antiphon*
Holy virgin Mary, there is no one in the world like you, no woman who has been born in the world is like you. You are the daughter and handmaid of the most high King, the heavenly Father. You are the mother of our most holy Lord Jesus Christ, spouse of the Holy Spirit. Pray for us, with St Michael the archangel and all the virtues of heaven and all the saints around your dear and most holy Son, our Lord and Master.

*Psalm (see Pss. 47; 96)*
O all ye nations, clap your hands, praise God with cries of gladness.

He is the Lord most high and terrible, the King of all the earth.

O most holy, heavenly Father, our King, who before all ages hath sent from on high his dear Son, hath wrought our salvation in the midst of the earth.

Let the heavens rejoice, let the earth be glad, let the sea leap with all that is in it: let the fields be joyful with all they bring forth.

Sing unto him a new song, let the earth praise the Lord.

For the Lord is great and worthy of praise: he is more to be feared than all gods.

Bring to the Lord, O ye kindreds of the Gentiles, bring to the Lord glory and honour, bring to the Lord the glory due to his name.

Bring your own bodies and bear his holy cross, and follow to the end his most holy precepts.

Let all the earth be moved at his presence, proclaim to all nations that the Lord hath reigned.

# 4

# THE OFFICE OF THE LORD'S PASSION FOR ADVENT UNTIL CHRISTMAS EVE

Here begin other psalms which our most blessed father
Francis also selected. They are to be said instead of the
preceding ones, from Advent until Christmas Eve, and no
longer.

## At Compline

*Antiphon*
Holy virgin Mary, there is no one in the world like you, no
woman who has been born in the world is like you. You
are the daughter and handmaid of the most high King, the
heavenly Father. You are the mother of our most holy
Lord Jesus Christ, spouse of the Holy Spirit. Pray for us,
with St Michael the archangel and all the virtues of heaven
and all the saints around your dear and most holy Son, our
Lord and Master.

*Psalm (see Ps. 13)*
How long, O Lord, wilt thou forget me unto the end?

How long wilt thou hide thy face from me?

How long shall I take counsel in my soul, having sorrow in my heart all the day?

How long shall my enemy be exalted over me? Consider and hear me, O Lord, my God.

Enlighten mine eyes that I sleep not in death, lest at any time my enemy say: I have prevailed against him. They that trouble me will rejoice when I am moved, but I have trusted in thy mercy.

My heart shall rejoice in thy salvation. I will sing unto the Lord, because he has dealt bountifully with me; yea, I will sing to the name of the Lord most high.

## At Matins

*Antiphon*
Holy virgin Mary, there is no one in the world like you, no woman who has been born in the world is like you. You are the daughter and handmaid of the most high King, the heavenly Father. You are the mother of our most holy Lord Jesus Christ, spouse of the Holy Spirit. Pray for us, with St Michael the archangel and all the virtues of heaven and all the saints around your dear and most holy Son, our Lord and Master.

*Psalm (see Ps. 118:14; 69:32–36; etc.)*
I will praise thee, O Lord, Father most holy, King of heaven and earth, because thou hast comforted me.

Behold, God is my Saviour. I will deal confidently and will not fear.

The Lord is my strength and my praise, and is become my salvation.

Thy right hand, O Lord, is magnified in strength; thy right hand, O Lord, hath slain the enemy, and in the multitude of thy glory thou hast put down my adversaries.

Let the poor see and rejoice; seek ye God, and your soul shall live.

Let the heavens and the earth praise him; the sea and everything that creepeth therein.

For God will save Sion, and the cities of Judah will he build up.

And men shall come and dwell there, and acquire it by inheritance.

And the seed of the servants of God shall possess it, and they that love his name shall dwell therein.

## At Prime

*Antiphon*
Holy virgin Mary, there is no one in the world like you, no woman who has been born in the world is like you. You are the daughter and handmaid of the most high King, the heavenly Father. You are the mother of our most holy Lord Jesus Christ, spouse of the Holy Spirit. Pray for us, with St Michael the archangel and all the virtues of heaven and all the saints around your dear and most holy Son, our Lord and Master.

*Psalm (see Ps. 57)*
Have mercy on me, O God, have mercy on me: for my soul trusteth in thee.

And in the shadow of thy wings will I hope, until iniquity pass away.

I will cry to God the most high: to God who hath done good to me.

He hath sent from heaven and delivered me, he hath covered my persecutors with shame.

God hath sent his power and his truth, he hath delivered my soul from the fury of mine enemies and of those who hated me: they made themselves strong against me.

They laid snares for my feet, and have threatened my life.

They dug a pit before my face, and they are fallen into it.

My heart is ready, O God, my heart is ready. I will sing and rehearse a psalm.

Arise, O my glory, arise psaltery and harp: I will arise early.

I will give praise to thee, O Lord, among the people: I will sing a psalm to thee among the nations.

For thy mercy is magnified even to the heavens, and thy truth unto the clouds.

Be thou exalted, O God, above the heavens, and thy glory above all the earth.

Glory be to the Father, and to the Son, and to the Holy Spirit. As it was in the beginning, is now, and ever shall be, world without end. Amen.

## At Terce

*Antiphon*
Holy virgin Mary, there is no one in the world like you, no woman who has been born in the world is like you. You are the daughter and handmaid of the most high King, the heavenly Father. You are the mother of our most holy Lord Jesus Christ, spouse of the Holy Spirit. Pray for us, with St Michael the archangel and all the virtues of heaven and all the saints around your dear and most holy Son, our Lord and Master.

*Psalm (see Pss. 17; 65; 72)*
Rejoice all before God, ye inhabitants of the earth, sing a psalm to his name, glorify him and praise him.

Say unto God, how terrible are thy works, O Lord! The greatness of thy power shall confound thine enemies.

Let all the earth adore thee and praise thee, let it sing a psalm to thy name.

Come and listen, all ye who fear the Lord, and I will tell

you what great things he hath done for my soul.

I opened my mouth and cried to him, my tongue hath extolled him.

He hath heard my voice from his holy temple, my cry has gone up to him.

Bless our Lord, ye nations, and let your voices be heard to praise him.

All the tribes of the earth shall be blessed in him, all nations shall exalt him.

Blessed be the Lord God of Israel, who only doeth wondrous things.

And blessed be the name of his majesty for ever, and the whole earth shall be filled with his majesty.

## At Sext

*Antiphon*

Holy virgin Mary, there is no one in the world like you, no woman who has been born in the world is like you. You are the daughter and handmaid of the most high King, the heavenly Father. You are the mother of our most holy Lord Jesus Christ, spouse of the Holy Spirit. Pray for us, with St Michael the archangel and all the virtues of heaven and all the saints around your dear and most holy Son, our Lord and Master.

*Psalm (see Pss. 10; 20; 59)*

May the Lord hear thee in the day of trouble, may the name of the God of Jacob protect thee.

May he send thee help from the sanctuary, and defend thee out of Sion.

May he be mindful of all thy sacrifices, and may thy wholeburnt offering be made fat.

May he fulfil the desires of thine heart, and confirm all thy counsels.

We will rejoice in thy salvation, and in the name of our

God we shall be exalted.

May the Lord look favourably on all thy petitions; now know I that the Lord hath sent his Son Jesus Christ, and that he will judge the people with justice.

The Lord is become a refuge for the poor, a helper of the needy and persecuted; and let them trust in thee who know thy name.

Blessed be the Lord my God, he is become my help and my refuge in the day of my tribulation.

O my helper, I will sing to thee: God is my help and my defence, my God, my mercy.


**At None**

*Antiphon*
Holy virgin Mary, there is no one in the world like you, no woman who has been born in the world is like you. You are the daughter and handmaid of the most high King, the heavenly Father. You are the mother of our most holy Lord Jesus Christ, spouse of the Holy Spirit. Pray for us, with St Michael the archangel and all the virtues of heaven and all the saints around your dear and most holy Son, our Lord and Master.


*Psalm (see Pss. 59; 69; 71)*
In thee, Lord, have I hoped, let me never be put to confusion; deliver me in thy justice, and rescue me.

Incline thine ear unto me, and save me.

Be thou unto me a God, a protector, and a place of strength, that thou mayest make me safe.

For thou art my patience, O Lord, my hope, Lord, from my youth.

Upon thee have I leaned from my mother's womb, thou art my protector ever since I was born: of thee shall I continually sing.

Let my mouth be filled with thy praise; that I may sing

thy glory and thy greatness all the day long.

Hear me, O Lord, for thy mercy is kind, look upon me according to the multitude of thy tender mercies.

And turn not away thy face from thy child, for I am in trouble; hear me speedily.

Blessed be the Lord my God; he is become my helper and my refuge in the day of my tribulation.

O my helper, I will sing to thee; God is my defence; my God, my mercy.


## At Vespers

*Antiphon*
Holy virgin Mary, there is no one in the world like you, no woman who has been born in the world is like you. You are the daughter and handmaid of the most high King, the heavenly Father. You are the mother of our most holy Lord Jesus Christ, spouse of the Holy Spirit. Pray for us, with St Michael the archangel and all the virtues of heaven and all the saints around your dear and most holy Son, our Lord and Master.


*Psalm (see Pss. 47; 96)*
O all ye nations, clap your hands, praise God with cries of gladness.

He is the Lord most high and terrible, the King of all the earth.

O most holy, heavenly Father, our King, who before all ages hath sent from on high his dear Son, hath wrought our salvation in the midst of the earth.

Let the heavens rejoice, let the earth be glad, let the sea leap with all that is in it: let the fields be joyful with all they bring forth.

Sing unto him a new song, let the earth praise the Lord.

For the Lord is great and worthy of praise: he is more to be feared than all gods.

Bring to the Lord, O ye kindreds of the Gentiles, bring to the Lord glory and honour, bring to the Lord the glory due to his name.

Bring your own bodies and bear his holy cross, and follow to the end his most holy precepts.

Let all the earth be moved at his presence, proclaim to all nations that the Lord hath reigned.

## At Vespers on the Lord's nativity

*Antiphon*
Holy virgin Mary, there is no one in the world like you, no woman who has been born in the world is like you. You are the daughter and handmaid of the most high King, the heavenly Father. You are the mother of our most holy Lord Jesus Christ, spouse of the Holy Spirit. Pray for us, with St Michael the archangel and all the virtues of heaven and all the saints around your dear and most holy Son, our Lord and Master.

*Psalm (see especially Pss. 47; 89; 108; 116)*
Let us magnify God our helper, let us sing to the true and living Lord God with shouts of gladness.

For he is a very great and terrible Lord, the supreme King of all the universe.

For our most holy, heavenly Father, our King from all eternity, hath sent from on high his only Son, who is born of the most blessed and holy virgin Mary.

He will say to me: thou art my Father, and I will proclaim him as my first-begotten Son, above the kings of the earth.

On this day the Lord God hath sent his mercy, and the night shall resound with his praises.

This is the day that the Lord hath made: let us rejoice and be glad in it.

For a dear and very holy child has been given to us, he

is born for us, on our road, he was placed in a manger, because there was no room in the inn.

Glory from the highest heaven to the Lord God, and on earth peace to men of good will.

Let the heavens rejoice, let the earth be glad, let the sea make a noise with all that is in it, let the fields be joyful with the fullness thereof.

Sing ye to the Lord a new canticle: let all the earth praise him.

For the Lord is great, and exceedingly to be praised: he is more terrible than all gods.

Bring to the Lord, O ye kindreds of the Gentiles, bring to the Lord glory and honour: bring to the Lord glory unto his name.

Prepare your bodies and bear his holy cross and follow to the end his most holy precepts.

(This psalm is said from Christmas to the Epiphany octave at all the Hours.)

# Part IV

# PRAYERS AND CANTICLES

# PRAYERS

## Prayer 'God almighty'

God almighty, eternal, just and merciful, grant to us, miserable sinners, grace to do for thee what we know to be thy will. May we desire what pleases you. May we be inwardly purified, inwardly enlightened and set on fire by the Holy Spirit. May we follow in the footsteps of thy Son, our Lord Jesus Christ and come to thee through thy grace alone. O most high God, thou livest in perfect trinity and absolute unity and reignest gloriously, God almighty, from everlasting to everlasting. Amen.

## Lauds

The praises which the most blessed father St Francis composed start here. He used to recite them at all hours of the day and night and before the Office of the most blessed virgin Mary. They begin with, 'Our Father, most holy,' and are followed by the Gloria and the praises, 'Holy, holy, holy,' etc.

*Explanation of the Lord's Prayer*
*Our Father* most holy, our Creator, Redeemer, Saviour and Comforter.
*Who art in heaven.* May thy kingdom shine in us so that we

may know the greatness of thy benefits, the breadth of thy promises, the height of thy majesty and the depth of thy judgements (see Eph. 3:18).

*Thy kingdom come.* So that thou mayest reign in us by thy grace and mayest make us enter into thy kingdom, where thou art clearly seen, where there is the perfect love of thee, the blessed company of thee, the eternal enjoyment of thee.

*Thy will be done in earth as it is in heaven.* How we love thee with all our heart, thinking always about thee; with our whole soul, desiring thee always; with our whole mind, directing all our thoughts towards thee. We seek your honour in everything. With all our strength we submit our faculties to thee. All our spirits and bodies we submit to only obeying your love. We will love our neighbours as ourselves. We will do our utmost to encourage the whole world to love thee. We rejoice with those who rejoice as if the good fortune had been our own. We sympathise with the sad and never offend anyone.

*Give us this day our daily bread.* Our Lord Jesus Christ, thy dear Son, reminds us of and makes us understand the love he has for us. He makes us venerate all that he has said, done and suffered for us.

*And forgive us our trespasses.* We are forgiven through thine ineffable mercy and by virtue of the passion of thy dear Son our Lord Jesus Christ. We are forgiven through the merits and intercession of the most blessed virgin Mary and of all thine elect.

*As we forgive them that trespass against us.* Grant, O Lord, that even though we do not completely forgive we may nevertheless be completely forgiven. May we truly love our enemies for thy sake; may we pray to thee devoutly for them and may we repay no one evil for evil. May we strive to be useful to every one for thy sake.

*And lead us not into temptation.* Lead us not into hidden or open temptations, or sudden or persistent temptations.

*But deliver us from evil.* Deliver us from past evil, present evil and future evil. Amen.

*Gloria*
Glory be to the Father and to the Son and to the Holy Spirit. As it was in the beginning, is now and ever shall be, world without end. Amen.

*Praises*
'Holy, holy, holy, Lord God almighty, who was, and who is, and who is to come' (Rev. 4:8). Praise him and exalt him above all for ever (see Dan. 3:57).

Worthy thou art to receive all praise, glory, honour and blessing (see Rev. 4:11). Praise him and exalt him above all for ever.

'The Lamb that was slain is worthy to receive power, and divinity, and wisdom, and strength, and honour, and glory and blessing' (Rev. 4:12).

Let us bless the Father, the Son and the Holy Spirit. Praise him and exalt him above all for ever.

'All ye works of the Lord, bless the Lord: praise and exalt him above all for ever' (Dan. 3:57).

'Give praise to our God, all ye his servants, and you that fear him little and great' (Rev. 19:5). Praise him and exalt him above all for ever.

Let heaven and earth, and 'every creature, which is in heaven, on the earth and under the earth, the sea and all that is in it, praise this glorious God' (see Rev. 5:13). Praise him and exalt him above all for ever.

Glory be to the Father, and to the Son, and to the Holy Spirit. Praise him and exalt him above all for ever. As it was in the beginning, is now, and ever shall be, world without end. Amen. Praise him and exalt him above all for ever.

*Prayer*
Sovereign God almighty, most holy and most high, supreme goodness, universal goodness, the absolute good thou art alone good. We offer thee all praise, all glory, all deeds of grace, all honour, all blessing, and we give thee thanks continually for all good which exists. Amen.

## A Greeting to the Blessed Virgin Mary

Hail, blessed lady, queen most holy, mother of God, Mary, perpetual virgin. You were chosen from the highest heaven by the most holy Father, consecrated by him and by his most holy, dear Son and by the Spirit, the Consoler. The fullness of grace and universal grace dwell in you. Hail, palace of God! Hail, temple of God! Hail, house of the Lord! Hail, clothing of the Lord! Hail, handmaid of the Lord! Hail, mother of God! Hail, all you holy virtues through which you infuse the heart of the faithful by the grace and illumination of the Holy Spirit. You make disciples of God out of faithless people.

## A Greeting to the Virtues

Greetings, O wisdom, O queen, may the Lord keep thee and thy sister simplicity, holy and pure. Lady holy poverty, may the Lord keep thee and thy most holy sister obedience. May the Lord keep all of you most holy virtues. You come from the Lord, your source. No person in the world can possess a single virtue unless he first dies to himself. A person who possesses one virtue will possess all the others provided that he does not harm any of them. A person who hurts one of the virtues offends them all and does not possess any of them.

Each virtue puts vices and sins to confusion. Holy wisdom confounds Satan and all his devices. Pure and holy simplicity confounds all worldly wisdom and all human wisdom. Holy poverty confounds all covetousness, avarice and conformity to this world. Holy humility confounds pride and all worldly men and all that is in the world. Holy charity confounds all diabolical and carnal temptations and all fear of nature. Holy obedience confounds all the desires of the body and of the flesh. Holy obedience keeps the body mortified so that it can obey the spirit and its brother. Holy obedience makes a person submissive to all people in the world. Holy obedience also makes a person submissive to animals, even wild animals, which can do as they wish with him, so long as it is granted to them from above by the Lord.

## Prayer for Love

Lord, I pray thee, that the burning and delicious ardour of thy love may detach my soul from all things which are under heaven, so that I may die for love of thy love. For thou art the One who for love of my love was prepared to die.

## Prayer in Time of Sickness

I give thee thanks, Lord God, for all the pains with which I am afflicted, and I pray thee, O my Lord, increase them a hundred times if that is thy will. For my great desire is that thou spare me not affliction nor torment. My supreme consolation is in the fulfilment of thy holy will.

## Prayer for Poverty

O Lord Jesus, show me the way of your very dear poverty. I know that the Old Testament was the figure of the New Testament. You did make this promise to the Jews, 'I will deliver to you every place that the sole of your foot shall tread upon' (Jos. 1:3). To tread underfoot means to scorn. For poverty tramples everything underfoot and so she is the universal queen. But, my sweet Lord Jesus Christ, have pity on me and on Lady Poverty, for I am tormented for love of her and I have no peace apart from her.

O my Lord, you know well that you have made me in

love with her and behold, she is full of sadness, and repulsed by everyone. She is like a widow who is the queen of nations. She is vile and despised who is the queen of all virtues. Seated on a dunghill she weeps and all her friends despise her. They behave as adulterers and not as faithful partners. Behold, Lord Jesus, poverty is the queen of virtues and for her you did leave the angelic throne when you came to earth. In your eternal love you have married her in order to have, by her, in her and of her perfect sons. She was so faithfully devoted to you that she began to serve you from your mother's womb by giving you the smallest of living bodies.

When you came forth from the Virgin's womb poverty welcomed you in the holy manger, in a stable. During your stay in the world poverty deprived you of all things so that you had nowhere to lay your head. As an inseparable companion poverty followed you faithfully as you began the battle for our salvation. In the middle of your passion poverty alone stood beside you like a squire. Your disciples forsook you and denied you but poverty faithfully stayed with you and supplied you with the whole escort of her sisters. Even your mother, who alone remained steadfastly attached to you and shared your passion with so much anguish, could not reach you on your raised cross. But Lady Poverty, with all her privations, like a gentle maiden embraced you more chastely than ever as she was so intimately united with you in your crucifixion. As usual, she took no trouble to polish and arrange the cross. Will anybody believe that she did not even provide enough nails for your crucifixion? The nails were not polished or sharp. She only prepared three nails and they were rough, big and blunt so that you suffered even more. While you were dying of thirst, this faithful spouse saw to it that you should be denied even a little water. She also made the impious soldiers offer you a drink that was too bitter to taste let alone drink. You gave up your soul in the tight embrace of this spouse.

But, faithful spouse, she did not leave you at the place where you were buried. She only allowed you to borrow the sepulchre, the spices and the linen. This holy spouse was not absent at your resurrection. She rejoiced in your kisses when you gloriously rose from the tomb as you left behind what you had been given or lent. Then you took her with you into the skies as you left to the world all that belongs to the world. To Lady Poverty you have given the seal of the kingdom of heaven which is used to mark out those people who wish to walk in the way of perfection.

Oh, who then would not love Lady Poverty above everything else? I implore you to be marked with her seal. I desire to be enriched by such a treasure. I swear to you, most poor Jesus, that on account of the love of your name I have no personal possessions. As long as I am alive in this miserable body I will always use sparingly the gifts other people offer me. So be it.

# CANTICLES

## The Canticle of the Sun

Most high, most great and good Lord, to thee belong praises, glory and every blessing; to thee alone do they belong, most high God. No one is worthy to call thee by thy name.

Blessed be thou, my Lord, for the gift of all thy creatures and especially for our brother, master sun, by whom the day is enlightened. He is radiant and bright, of great splendour, bearing witness to thee, O my God.

Blessed be thou, my Lord, for our sister the moon and the stars; thou hast formed them in the heavens, fair and clear.

Blessed be thou, my Lord, for my brother the wind, for the air, for cloud and calm, for every kind of weather, for through them thou sustainest all creatures.

Blessed be thou, my Lord, for our sister water, which is very useful, humble, chaste and precious.

Blessed be thou, my Lord, for brother fire, bright, noble and beautiful, untamable and strong, by whom thou illuminest the night.

Blessed be thou, my Lord, for our mother the earth, who sustains and nourishes us, who brings forth all kinds of fruit, herbs and brightly coloured flowers.

Blessed be thou, my Lord, for those who pardon for love of thee, and who patiently bear infirmity and tribulation.

Happy are those who abide in peace, for by thee, most high God, they will be crowned.

Blessed be thou, my Lord, for our sister death of body, from whom no living man can escape. Woe to him who dies in a state of mortal sin. Happy are those who at the hour of death are found in obedience to thy holy will, for the second death cannot hurt them.

Praise ye and bless ye my Lord; give him thanks and serve him with great humility.

['My sisters the birds,' St Francis also said, 'you ought always to love the Lord your Creator, and praise him much. He has given you feathers to clothe you and everything else that you need as well as the wings with which you fly. God has made you noble among creatures as you live in the middle of the pure air. You do not sow and you do not reap and yet you are delivered from all care. God protects and directs you.']

## The Canticle of the Furnace

[In order to appreciate this canticle and the following one it must be remembered that the saints live a life of pure love, receiving only God's pure love. As in the Song of Songs the motive which explains their burning accents is the pure love of God.]

Love has set me in a furnace, he has set me in a furnace of love.

My new spouse, the loving Lamb, has given me the nuptial ring. He has imprisoned me, smitten me with a lance and pierced my heart.

He has pierced my heart and my body has fallen to the ground. The arrows fired from his bow of love have struck me. He has turned peace into war and I am dying of sweetness.

I am dying of sweetness, do not wonder about that. These strokes have been made by a loving lance. The sword is long and wide and it has pierced me through and through.

Then the darts showered on me so thickly that I nearly died. Then I took a shield but the blows increased so much that I could no longer protect myself. They wounded me all over my body, so strong was the arm that hurled them.

He hurled them with such strength that I despaired of parrying them, and to avoid death I cried with all my strength, 'Thou art breaking the laws of chivalry.' But the Father equipped the Son with a war machine which overwhelmed me with fresh blows.

The darts which Christ threw were stones covered with lead weighing many thousand pounds. They rained on me like thick hail and I was unable to count them. None of them missed me.

Christ never missed me once since he was so good at throwing them. My limbs were unable to come to my assistance as I was lying on the ground. My body was bruised and broken and I had no more feeling than a dead man has.

I was dead, not on account of death, but because of joy. After I recovered the use of my body I became so strong that I could follow the guides who conducted me to heaven's gates.

After I regained my strength I immediately armed myself. I waged war on Christ and invaded his territory. As soon as I met up with him I fought against him and took my revenge on him.

After I had taken my revenge I made a pact with him since Christ had loved me from the beginning with a true love. Now my heart is able to receive the consolations of Christ.

Love has set me in a furnace. He has set me in a furnace of love.

**The Canticle of Love**

Love of loves, why have you so wounded me? My heart, torn from its dwelling, is consumed with love.

It is on fire, it burns, it finds no resting place, it cannot flee because it is chained up. It is consumed like wax in the fire. Dying it lives. Its languor is sweet, it prays for power to escape for a while and finds itself in the middle of a furnace. Alas, where will this terrible faintness lead me? The burning heat of this fire so stifles me that it is death to live like this.

Before making trial of it, I prayed to Christ asking for his love. I thought that I would find sweetness in his love and that I would delight in his gentle peace so much that no worries would be able to trouble me. But I experienced a torment that I could never have imagined. The heat breaks my heart. I cannot describe how I suffer. I am dying of sweetness and I live deprived of my heart.

My heart, wounded by divine love, is no longer my own. I have no judgement, no will, no ability to enjoy myself or sense of feeling. All beauty seems to be like mud and delights and riches are perdition. A tree of love, laden with fruit, is planted in my heart and nourishes me. It transforms me so much that it expels my self-will, intelligence and strength.

I have entirely renounced both the world and myself in order to buy love. If I owned all of creation I would gladly trade that for love. But I find that love has deceived me. I have given everything and yet I do not know where I am being drawn to. Love has destroyed me. I am looked at as if I am mad, and because I have been sold, I am no longer worth anything.

The world and the friends who are outside this realm of love tried to bring me back to them. But the person who has once given himself cannot give himself a second time. The servant cannot be the master. A stone will become soft more quickly than love will stop holding me. My complete will is burnt up with love, is united to it, transformed into it and consumed by it.

I shall not be separated from love by either fire or sword. It is impossible to divide this union. Suffering and death cannot rise to the height to which love lures me. Outside this union all created things are restless and through it the soul is raised above everything. O my soul, through what happy chance do you possess such blessings? They come to you from Christ. Therefore embrace him with sweetness.

I am unable to look at any creature without my whole soul praising the Creator. Neither heaven nor earth holds anything dear to me. Everything is swept away by the love of Christ. The sun's light seems dark when I behold Christ's dazzling face. The cherubim, who excel in knowledge, and the seraphim who excel in love both lose their beauty for the person who sees the Lord.

Let no one reproach me if such a love makes me mad. No heart is capable of defending itself or fleeing from these chains of love. Can you imagine a heart not suffering and breaking in such a furnace? Oh, if I could only find a soul to understand me, to take pity on me and know all my heart's anguish!

Heaven and earth and all creation cries out to me that I must love. Everything says to me, 'With all thy heart love the Love which loves thee, love the Love which desires thee, and has created thee to draw thee wholly to himself.' Therefore I desire never to stop drawing on this holy light and this ineffable goodness which is spread around.

If I was able to love more I would, but my heart can love no more. Clearly, I cannot give more than myself, even if I desire to give more than that. I have given everything to possess this Lover who has made a new man of me since I found him. O goodness old and always new, immense Light whose splendour is so sweet!

At the sight of so much beauty I am transported outside myself without knowing where I am being taken to. My heart softens like melted wax and Christ's form is traced on it. Never before has such a change come over me. I have stripped myself to be clothed in Christ. My heart is transformed and its cry is love. My soul is consumed with heavenly delights. My happily chained soul rushes to the embrace of the Well-beloved. The more my soul beholds Christ's beauty the more it is beside itself. Rich in Christ it loses everything in him. It no longer recalls anything about itself. It no longer strives to gain anything at all, it is incapable of losing anything and it no longer feels anything.

Transformed in Christ it has almost become Christ. United to God it is entirely divine. God's magnificent riches surpass all grandeur. Christ reigns supreme in the soul. Can I therefore remain sad and beg a remedy for my faults? I no longer possess an abyss full of sin in me. The old man is dead and has been robbed of all his impurities.

In Christ a new creature is born. The old man is taken away and I have become a new man. But love is so strong that it is as if my heart is split in two by a sword. This fire consumes my soul and my mind. In his beauty Christ completely allures me. I am on fire when I see him. I utter a cry of love, 'O Love, the height of my desire, let me die of love!'

For thee, O Love, I waste and languish, I go about uttering cries and seeking thy kisses. When you go my life becomes death and I sigh and pine to find thee. When thou returnest my heart enlarges because in thee it can be entirely transformed. Then delay no more, O Love; be mindful of me, thou holdest me in chains, consume my heart.

Sweet Love, consider my trouble. I can bear such ardour no longer. Love has taken possession of me. I no longer know where I am and I no longer know what I am saying or doing. I travel along the road like a lost man. I collapse exhausted from languor. I do not know how to bear such torment. The grief it gives me has ravished my heart.

My heart is enraptured, and I can no longer see what I have to do or what I have not to do. People who observe me ask if a love without deeds can please thee, O Christ. If it does not please you what can I do? My heart is worn out with abundance of Christ's love. Love, which enfolds me, takes away all action and all initiative. I lose all sense of feeling.

Before, I knew how to speak; now, I am dumb. Before, I could see; now, I am blind. There has never been such a great capture. I am silent, and I speak; I fly, and I am chained; I fall, and I am raised up; I hold, and I am held. All at the same moment I am inside and outside; I pursue and I am pursued. Insensate Love, why dost thou make me mad, why dost thou kill me in such a raging furnace?

*Christ*
Control your love, you who love me. There is no virtue without order. Since you desire so much to find me renew your soul through virtue. I truly wish that you should call upon me as you love me, although your love must be disciplined. The tree is known by the goodness of its fruit. Law presides over everything and gives everything its value.

Everything that I have made has harmony and proportion and is ordained to a particular end. Order guards them. Charity, more than any other virtue, naturally wants to be regulated. Are you, O soul, by your ardour, being foolish? Your fervour is not curbed because it has no control on it.

*The soul*
O Christ, you have ravished my heart, and you say to my soul, 'Control your love!' Since I am transformed into you how is it possible for me to master myself. As the iron turns red in the fire and as in the translucent air the sun's rays lose their form and assume another shape, so is the pure soul entirely transformed with your love.

Since it has lost its own virtue it is powerless to act by itself. It becomes like this because of its virtue. These are the deeds and fruits it produces. If then it is transformed into your truth and yourself alone, O Christ, whom it is so sweet to love, it is to you and not to myself that my deeds must be imputed. If I cease to please you, O Love, it is because you are no longer pleasing to yourself.

If it is true that I am mad, O supreme Wisdom, the fault is yours. It dates from the day when you wounded me and I made a pact with Love. My self has been taken away and I am clothed in you. I do not know how I was drawn to a new life. I was in utter dejection but love has made me strong. The gates are broken down and I live with you, O Love.

Why have you led me into such a furnace if it is your will that I should keep within bounds? In giving yourself to me without measure you have taken all measure from me. Since I am small you fully satisfy me and as you are great I cannot possess you any more. If this is foolishness, O Love, it comes from you and not from me. You, O Love, have directed me along this path.

You have not forbidden yourself to love. It was love that made you come from heaven to earth, O Love. You came in such great humility that you walked the earth like a despised man. You did not desire a place to live or possessions to own and we are made rich through this poverty. In life and in death you gave unmistakable signs of the boundless love which consumed your heart.

You went through the world like a man who is beside himself. Love led you like a slave. In everything, O Love, you showed that you did not think of yourself. At the door of the temple you cried, 'Let him who has suffered the thirst of love, come and drink; he shall be given a boundless love which will satisfy and console him.'

Wisdom has not prevented you from ceaselessly spreading your love abroad. To save us, O incarnate love, you were born of love and not of the flesh. To inflame us with love you went to the cross. When you did not defend yourself before Pilate it was in order to bring about our redemption on the cross of love.

I see that wisdom hid itself and love alone was visible. Power no longer showed itself and strength ceased to give pleasure. The love which poured itself out in this way was great. In his look and in his heart were no other thoughts than loving sentiments. As love was bound on the cross so mankind was embraced by an immense love.

O Jesus, I am so full of love and inebriated with so much sweetness. So who can blame me or reproach me if I live like a madman without any will, feeling or strength? Love has constrained you and robbed you of all your majesty. So who then can prevent me from going mad to embrace you, O my Love?

This love which has made me mad really seems to have taken wisdom from you. This love in which I languish has deprived you of all power because of me. I am a captive to love and can resist no longer. The decree has gone out that I shall die of love. I do not want any other consolation than to die of love.

Love, Love who has so wounded me, I can only utter one cry, 'Love!' I am united to you by love and love embraces you in me. Love, Love, who has so wounded me, my heart grows weaker and weaker with love. I am absorbed in you, O Love. Let me abide with you and in your goodness let me die of love.

Love, Love, O Jesus, I am reaching the haven. Love, Love, O Jesus, receive me. Love, Love, O Jesus, come to my help. It is love, love for Jesus which inflames me thus. Love, Love, O Jesus, I am dying of love, let me be near you. O Love, embrace me always; transform me into yourself, O Love, into truth, into supreme charity.

Love, Love, it is the cry of the whole world. Love, Love, it is the cry of everything. Love, Love, such is your depth, that the more one is bound to you the more one desires you. Love, Love, you are the circle that surrounds my heart; he who possesses you loves you for ever. You are my food and my clothing. The person who loves you is so happy to possess you, to feel your presence, that he cries unceasingly, 'Love!'

Love, Love, you make me suffer so much that I cannot bear it any longer. Love, Love, you have such dominion over me. Transform me into yourself. Love, sweet languor; Love, my desire; Love, my delight bind me with love.

Love, Love, my heart is broken and is seriously wounded. Love, draw me towards your beauty as I am ravished by you. Love, Love, do not disdain me as you are my life. Oh, do not forsake me as you have made me faint with love.

In this anguish of Love, Love, Love, O my adorable Jesus, I would die while embracing you, O Jesus, my sweet spouse. Love, Love, I beg for death from you; O pitying Jesus receive me and transform me into thyself. Remember that I am passing away killing myself with love. I do not know where I am. Jesus, my hope, destroy me with love.